P9-CJT-312

Better Homes and Gardens®

Celebrate

Volume 4

contents

summer

90 ENJOY the best of summer with decor ideas for both inside and outside your home. Discover garden art that's sure to bring giggles, indoor inspiration destined to bump up your style a notch, and holiday salutes that bring more meaning to the day than ever before. Your family and friends will thank you for the good times.

boo!

114 CONJURE up some wickedly awesome foods and decorations that are more irresistible than eerie. You'll be all set for your next Halloween party with all these doable ideas. From treat holders for the little ones to clever ideas for the grown-up ghouls, there's a little something for everyone in this pumpkin-time chapter.

easy does it

RELAX—these awesome crafts are quick to do, but are just as nifty as the store-bought variety and a whole lot more personal.

Celebrate
Volume 4

MEREDITH CONSUMER MARKETING
Vice President, Consumer Marketing: Janet Donnelly
Consumer Marketing Product Director: Heather Sorensen
Consumer Marketing Product Manager: Wendy Merical
Business Director: Ron Clingman
Senior Production Manager: Al Rodruck

WATERBURY PUBLICATIONS, INC.
Contributing Editor: Sue Banker
Contributing Art Director: Cathy Brett
Contributing Copy Editor: Terri Fredrickson
Contributing Proofreader: Gretchen Kauffman

Editorial Director: Lisa Kingsley
Creative Director: Ken Carlson
Associate Editors: Tricia Bergman, Mary Williams
Associate Design Director: Doug Samuelson
Production Assistant: Mindy Samuelson

BETTER HOMES AND GARDENS® MAGAZINE
Editor in Chief: Gayle Goodson Butler
Executive Editor: Oma Blaise Ford
Managing Editor: Gregory H. Kayko
Creative Director: Michael D. Belknap
Senior Deputy Editor, Food and Entertaining: Nancy Wall Hopkins

MEREDITH NATIONAL MEDIA GROUP
President: Tom Harty

MEREDITH CORPORATION
Chairman and Chief Executive Officer: Stephen M. Lacy

In Memoriam: E.T. Meredith III (1933–2003)

Copyright© 2014 by Meredith Corporation.
Des Moines, Iowa.
First Edition. All rights reserved.
Printed in the United States of America.
ISSN: 300426   ISBN: 978-0-696-30184-1

change is good

I have a friend, a very dear friend, who has the touch. Every time I walk into her condo, I feel it. That welcoming, interesting, fresh, feel-good ambience.

Not only is she an immaculate housekeeper, but she's always changing things up a bit. Fresh colors, hints of holiday wonder, a new bite to try. She doesn't save those special efforts for only the big end-of-the-year holidays; she embraces them all year long. I cherish every visit.

That's what *Better Homes and Gardens® Celebrate* is all about. It's bringing that welcoming feeling into your own home through incredibly clever decorating ideas and foods that leave guests wanting seconds. It's about ALL the holidays and special moments that make life so very grand.

Celebrate helps you honor the special people in your life with unforgettable meals, fantastic parties, and endearing gifts. And when they visit your home, they'll enjoy your decorating efforts just as you do every day.

We hope these pages offer you new techniques, recipes, and inspiration so you too can switch it up a bit. You'll be amazed at how many kudos you get when you serve a delicious new dish or fill your home with accents to highlight the season. You'll be a hero, more so than you already are.

Here's to new adventures,

Sue Banker

LET THE YEAR
begin
A CLEAN SLATE

CHANGE THINGS UP

Give in to your decorator self. This chapter inspires new possibilities for your home as well as start-of-the-year celebrations.

Pillow Perks

Change the look of a room in an instant with fresh new pillows that set the tone.

Stylized Botanical

With its spindly form and distinctive blooms, the sarsaparilla plant comes to life in textural embroidery stitches.

WHAT YOU'LL NEED
fabric pen or pencil
tracing paper
8-inch embroidery hoop
natural linen (plain weave or twill): one
    24-inch square (pillow front) and two
    16×20-inch rectangles (pillow back)
crewel wool thread: 1 skein each of
    Appleton #441, #442, #443, #445,
    #481, #992
chenille needle: size 24, or comparable
    crewel needle of your choice
white cotton fabric for lining: one
    20-inch square and two 16×20-inch
    rectangles
hand-sewing needle
sewing thread
18-inch square pillow form
scissors
straight pins
ruler

WHAT YOU DO
1. Enlarge and trace pattern, page 154, onto center of linen square. Hoop the pillow front.
2. Refer to diagrams on page 155 for each stitch. Stitch stem and branches using chain stitch and #445. Split-stitch the leaves, alternating the uses of #441, #442, and #443. Stitch each blossom using circular couching stitch and #992 (see diagrams, above right) and double-wrapped French knots on ends. Use quadruple-wrapped French knots and #481 for flower centers.
3. Block finished crewelwork.
4. Trim 2 inches from each side of pillow front, leaving a 1-inch-wide border on all sides. The linen fabric with finished crewelwork should measure 20 inches square.
5. Lay crewelwork facedown on flat surface. Lay the 20-inch square lining piece on top of crewelwork. Pin the two pieces of fabric together and hand-baste using a series of 1- to 2-inch-long straight stitches in diagonal rows spaced about 3 inches apart. Stitch loosely so stitches will be easy to remove later; set aside.
6. Lay one 16×20-inch linen rectangle on

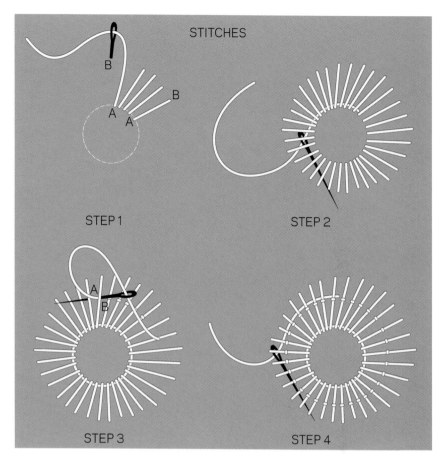

STITCHES

STEP 1

STEP 2

STEP 3

STEP 4

flat surface. Place one of the 16×20-inch lining pieces on top of the linen rectangle. Pin together and baste as in Step 5.
7. For each pillow back piece, fold one long edge 1½ inches in toward the lining. Press with a hot iron or finger-press. Fold in again another 1½ inches, press, and pin along the folded edge.
8. Using sewing thread, blanket-stitch along inside folded edge on back piece.
9. Lay basted and lined crewelwork faceup on a flat surface. Lay one of the small pieces facedown on top of the crewelwork with folds in middle and left edges lining up. Pin left edges together. Lay other small piece in the same manner, matching right side edges of the crewelwork; pin edges together. The two folded and hemmed edges overlap in center.
10. Pin the top and bottom edges; place a few pins through the center where the two smaller pieces overlap. Flip work so the lining side of the crewelwork is facing up.
11. Machine-sew the three pieces together, leaving a 1-inch hem on all sides; remove pins.

12. Trim the seam allowance to ½ inch. Snip corners, being careful not to cut too close to the seam; remove the basting stitches. Turn the pillow right side out.
13. Using the end of a blunt scissors, a knitting needle, or chopsticks, gently push out corners from inside the pillow. Slip the pillow insert into the opening in the back of the pillow cover and adjust as necessary.

STITCHES
1. Stitch a series of straight stitches that share the edge of a circle.
2. Lace thread underneath straight stitches and pull it to form a circle.
3. Bring needle up next to center of a straight stitch (A), bring thread over straight stitch, and then go back down on other side of stitch (B) to tack down straight stitch.
4. Lace thread underneath each straight stitch, outside the stitches from Step 3. Pull thread to form an outer circle.

Perfect Spot Pillow

Put a chair or sofa in the spotlight with a mod pillow. Layer felt circles and stitch them to the pillow front through the centers to create a lively graphic look.

WHAT YOU'LL NEED

two 13×17-inch pieces of linen: gray (pillow front and back)
three 11×14-inch pieces each of felt: orange, light purple, purple
sewing thread in orange, lavender, and gray
polyester fiberfill
sewing needle

WHAT YOU DO

1. Trace patterns, 155, onto white paper; cut out.

2. From orange felt cut: 5 large circles, 8 medium circles, and 9 small circles. From light purple felt cut: 8 large circles, 8 medium circles, and 9 small circles. From purple felt cut: 7 large circles, 8 medium circles, and 8 small circles.

3. Referring to Appliqué Placement Diagram, right, group same-size circles in pairs as shown. Fold the top circle in half and press the fold line. Open the circle and place it back on top of the matching circle.

4. Lay pillow front faceup on work surface. Refer to placement diagram to arrange circle pairs on pillow front; pin in place. Turn circle pairs so creases alternate horizontally and vertically.

5. Starting at center and working toward edges of pillow front, topstitch each felt circle pair to the pillow front, using the crease lines as guides for stitching. Trim thread ends.

6. Lay pillow back with right side down on pillow front. Refer to Pillow Assembly Diagram to sew pieces together using ½-inch seam allowance and leaving a 4-inch opening along the bottom edge. Firmly stuff the pillow with polyester fiberfill through the opening. Slipstitch opening closed.

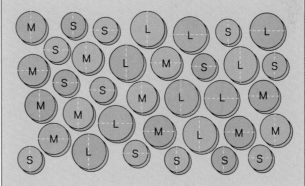

APPLIQUÉ PLACEMENT DIAGRAM

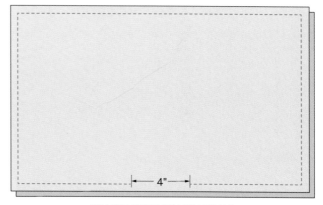

PILLOW ASSEMBLY DIAGRAM

Rip and Stitch

Got scraps? Pull them out and tear them into strips. You'll have fun creating a pillow from them.

WHAT YOU'LL NEED

scraps of assorted prints in blue, black, orange, pink, red, and purple (pillow top, ball trims)
26×21-inch piece of solid blue fabric (foundation)
polyester fiberfill

WHAT TO DO

Cut fabrics

Tear or cut fabrics in the following order (tearing the strips adds more texture to their edges). Circle Pattern A is on page 155.

From assorted blue, black, orange, pink, red, and purple prints, tear: enough 21-inch-long strips ranging in widths from ¼ to 1½ inches to cover foundation

From remaining prints, cut: 10 of Circle Pattern A or ten 2¾-inch-diameter circles

ASSEMBLE PILLOW TOP

1. Referring to Diagram 1, sew a 1½-inch-wide strip at one short edge of solid blue 26×21-inch rectangle, aligning raw edges and stitching ¼ inch from aligned edges. Repeat to add a second 1½-inch-wide strip on opposite edge of rectangle.
2. Starting from left edge, place a strip of desired width so it slightly overlaps edge of first strip (Diagram 2); pin in place. Stitch ⅛ inch to ¼ inch from overlapping edge.
3. Repeat Step 2, adding strips one at a time and working from left to right until solid blue rectangle is covered with strips, to make pillow top (Diagram 3).
4. Referring to photo and Diagram 4, sew narrower, shorter strips randomly to pillow top, trimming lengths as desired and stitching down center of each new strip.

5. To add more texture to pillow top, use your fingertips to rough up edges of strips. Trim long threads.

MAKE PILLOW

1. Fold pillow top in half with right side inside to make a 26×10½-inch rectangle (Diagram 5).
2. Sew together along long edge and one short edge. Turn right side out. Stuff firmly with polyester fiberfill.
3. Turn under raw edge ¼ inch; hand-sew opening closed to make pillow.

MAKE AND ADD BALL TRIMS

1. Using matching thread, sew a running stitch ½ inch from edge on right side of a print A circle as shown on Diagram 6 and Running Stitch Diagram.
2. Pull running stitch slightly, leaving thread on needle.
3. Stuff circle with enough fiberfill to make a small ball.
4. Pull running stitch tightly; backstitch. Wrap thread around gathered raw edge and backstitch again several times to make one ball trim.
5. Repeat Steps 1–4 to make a total of 10 ball trims.
6. Referring to photo, add five ball trims to one short end of pillow, stitching through rounded top of each ball trim and spacing ball trims evenly across pillow end. Repeat along opposite end to complete pillow.

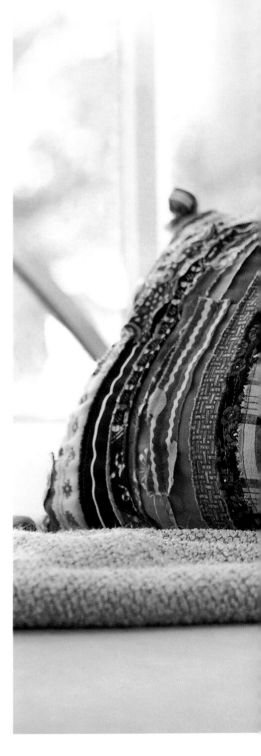

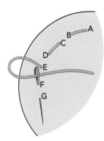

RUNNING STITCH

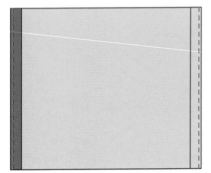

DIAGRAM 1

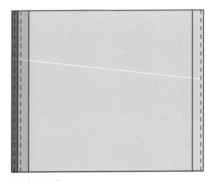

DIAGRAM 2

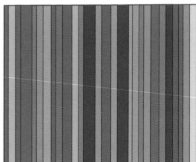

DIAGRAM 3

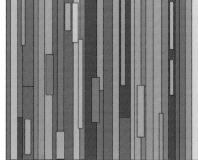

DIAGRAM 4

DIAGRAM 5

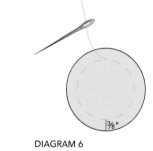

DIAGRAM 6

The Big Game

Whether you're huddled around the television or having pre-kickoff fun in the parking lot, you'll be on the winning tailgate team with these easy game-day ideas.

Go Team

Vintage or new, team buttons jazz up baskets to hold napkins, foods, silverware, and more. Add a ribbon bow and the servers are party ready

Apple of Everyone's Eye

Caramel apples are a treat in themselves. To dress them for the game, tie each stick with ribbons in one team color and add dimensional paper stickers in another. Serve on turf-green paper plates topped with a waxed paper square to avoid sticking.

Sports Bag

Football-theme candy makes a nice snack during the game or a fun take-home favor after the final whistle blows. Place candy into a clear cellophane bag and tie with ribbons in your favorite team's colors. From the bag, dangle a scrapbooking charm, such as this "spirit" dog tag.

Team Pride

There won't be any question whose side you're on when you spell it out, literally. Press alphabet stickers in a collegiate font along the edge of game-theme paper napkins and voila—coasters!

Hugs and Kisses

Easy on time yet big on sentiment, these Valentine's Day remembrances extend heartfelt wishes.

Hugs and Kisses Box

Craft a treasure box laden with Xs and Os. It's a fun gift in itself, or tuck a small gift inside for an added surprise for your Valentine.

WHAT YOU'LL NEED

cardboard recipe box or other desired size
instant glue, such as C1
varying sizes of washers and finishing washers
X-shape tile spacers in three sizes
dropcloth or newspaper
plastic bag
silver spray paint
decoupage medium
paintbrush
pink glitter
X and O ribbon
hot-glue gun and glue stick

WHAT YOU DO

1. Following the glue manufacturer's instructions and using the photo as a guide, glue washers on the left side of the lid and spacers on the right. Let glue dry.
2. In a well-ventilated work area, place box bottom in bag to avoid spray paint. Spray-paint the lid silver using two or three light coats and allowing to dry between coats. Let final coat dry and remove bag.
3. Use paintbrush to coat the sides of the box bottom with decoupage medium. While wet, sprinkle with glitter. Coat one side of a tile spacer with decoupage medium and sprinkle with glitter. Let decoupage medium dry.
4. Tie a ribbon bow and hot-glue to right side of box lid as shown. Glue a washer to bow center and top with glittered tile spacer.

Love Is All You Need

Dimensional cards have that extra-special something that won't soon be forgotten. To make a Valentine, purchase small alphabet buttons that spell out something appropriate for the holiday, such as "love," "heart," "be mine," or "always." Remove the wire from the back of the pin using pliers. Hot-glue the letters to the front of a piece of cardstock. Cut pieces of silver metallic chenille stem to frame each letter; hot-glue in place. Trim the cardstock and layer onto silver paper; trim a narrow border. Repeat with red glitter paper and white cardstock. Use strong double-sided tape to adhere the layers together.

Hats Off to Cupid

No one will guess that this treat holder was rescued from the recycle bin! Once a castaway cardboard ribbon spool, it transforms into a sparkling top hat with a little glitter and ribbon. Carefully tear off one cardboard end from spool as shown in Photo A. Use scissors to trim off rough edge as shown in Photo B. Paint the outside of the shape with decoupage medium and sprinkle with silver glitter as shown in Photo C. Tie a satin ribbon around the top and press a scrapbooking sticker to the center of the bow. Line the hat with clear cellophane before inserting the treats.

Love Notes

Remember your little sweetie on Valentine's Day too! Tuck a button-adorned card into a lunchbox for a fun midday surprise. To make a card, start with a 6×10-inch piece of printed cardstock. In the lower left corner, use a circle cutter to cut a hole large enough to frame a Valentine's Day button, leaving a ½-inch border at the left and bottom edges. Fold the cardstock in half, short ends together. Use a piece of double-sided tape to adhere ribbon extending from the top of the circle to the fold. Secure the pin to the inside of the card so that it is centered through the circular cutout. Write the desired message in the card.

Candy Hearts

Purchased candies in a heart-shape box make a wonderful Valentine's Day gift. To personalize the container, trace the lid onto adhesive-back glitter paper and cut out. Peel off the backing and adhere the paper to the lid. To finish the edge, attach ½-inch pom-poms with hot glue.

Presentation Plus

Dinner with your Valentine is a bit more romantic when place settings get a little nudge from Cupid. Layer metallic plate chargers in silver and red and top with paper heart doilies in two sizes. Use clear glass plates on top to let all the fun show through and tape a generous ribbon bow to one side.

Button, Button

Get out the button jar. You're about to craft some extra-special accessories for your home.

Posy Magnets

Pressed-paper flowers from the crafts store get even more dimensional with layered-button centers. Hot-glue the pieces together and glue a round magnet on the back. For an unexpected memo board, use a tart mold, taping the insert to the back side to allow the cutout shape to show.

Lovely Linens

Perk up place mats, napkins, and tablecloths with the addition of buttons and lazy daisy stitches. Use embroidery floss to secure several sizes of buttons to the fabric. For interest, try using French knots to secure some of the buttons. Surround a few of the buttons with lazy daisy stitches to resemble flower petals. Pin a ribbon bow to the base of the flowers and remove before laundering. The stitch diagrams are on page 155.

No-Sew Buttons

Whether you want to add a band of buttons to a shirt, curtains, or across a pillow—here's an easy way to get the look without a single stitch. Hot-glue the flat side of a button to a cork to make a stamp. Dip the button into fabric paint and gently press onto fabric. Follow the paint manufacturer's instructions to set the paint.

Cheery Plant Pokes

A green houseplant gets a splash of color with flowerlike buds bursting from it. Thread three or four buttons onto a sturdy crafts wire stem. Make a U shape at one end and feed the wire through the opposite hole in each of the buttons; bend or twist wire to secure.

Nostalgic Napkin Ring

Personalize a plain napkin ring with a piece of fabric measuring tape (or ribbon) and embroidery floss, then top with a special button. Use double-sided tape to hold ribbon on napkin ring, covering entire surface of ring. Wrap area where ribbons butt together with embroidery floss. Bring floss ends to the front of the napkin ring and knot. Thread a button onto floss ends, knot, and clip floss ends. To set a super-interesting table, use different ribbons, embroidery floss colors, and buttons to assemble each napkin ring.

Vintage-Style Frame

An ordinary frame is given old-fashioned appeal with the
addition of ribbon and a handful of buttons. Hot-glue strips
of ribbon around each frame side, wrapping from opening to
back edge. Cluster buttons on the lower right side of the
frame and glue in place. Before inserting photo, place a piece
of ribbon vertically into frame, holding it in place with the
glass insert.

Top o' the Gift

Remember your favorite Irishman with a gift on St. Patty's Day. Wrap the gift in green paper and trim with ribbon and a paper strip. Make a tag by cutting shape from green paper. Use a circle cutter to make a ½-inch circle and adhere it to narrow end of tag using glue stick. Punch a hole in the center. Cut a narrow strip of paper to embellish the end of the tag; glue in place. Use hot glue to attach four large green plastic gems in the shape of a four-leaf clover. Draw a stem with black marking pen. Thread ribbon through the hole and tie it to the package.

Pure Luck

The luck of the Irish be with you! Celebrate St. Patty's Day with party decor in coordinating shades of green

Claim It

Add a celebratory touch to beverages while marking the owners' glasses at the same time. To make a tag, cut a ½×10-inch strip of paper. Cross the tails and secure with an adhesive dot. Adhere a round frame to the center and top with a paper circle. Press an adhesive letter to the center. Use glue dots to hold the temporary glass embellishment in place.

Come on Over

Here's a stylish way to invite guests over on St. Patrick's Day. To make classy invitations, cut a 3½-inch square from white cardstock. Arrange four large green plastic gems in the shape of a clover and hot-glue to card. Draw a stem using black marking pen. Cut a 4-inch square from solid green cardstock, a 5-inch square from patterned green paper, and a 6×12-inch rectangle from medium green cardstock. Fold the rectangle in half, short ends together. Layer the pieces on the card front and adhere with glue stick.

Give Swirl a Whirl

If you like your home decor with a twist, try these simple and sophisticated marbling techniques to transform wall art, textiles, furniture, and more.

Tubes

Like a swirl of frosting atop a cupcake, a bit of marbling sweetens this tablescape. The paper pendants, place mats, and embellished glasses all employ the technique. These dangling paper tubes couldn't be easier: Simply marble paper using the how-to steps, page 29. When dry, roll each piece of paper into a tube and secure the seam with double-sided tape. Punch two tiny holes directly across from each other at the top. Thread the holes with fishing line, then use the line to suspend the tubes from removable hooks. For the glasses, use painter's tape to mask the sides, then carefully drip nail polish onto the outside bottoms of the glasses. Use a toothpick to swirl to your desired effect. Allow the nail polish to dry before removing the tape. Create custom place mats for your guests by marbling purchased place mats the same way as paper. Use cloth place mats, not vinyl or plastic, and avoid those with a shiny coating.

Ocean Tide

For wall art, marble paper using the technique on page 29 and wrap artist canvas with your creations. Use seashore colors to get the effect shown here or use your own color scheme.

Paper to Pillow

Throw together this simple-sew pillow in no time at all. After making marbled papers for wall pieces, scan the swirly image onto the computer and send your design off to a custom-fabric printing service. When the fabric arrives, use it to sew a simple pillow, allowing the gorgeous fabric to shine.

Curtain

Like the pillows on page 27, this curtain is a simple panel stitched from custom-designed fabric. Sew a rod casing and hem the edges and your art is ready to hang—window side!

Shelf Backer

Nail polish is the surprise ingredient for "marbling" slick surfaces, such as this medium density fiberboard (MDF). Pour 2 inches of water in a shallow container larger than the surface of your wall art. The container can be glass, aluminum, or plastic. Pour a thin film of fingernail polish on top of the water. (Tip: Use new polish; polish from old or open bottles tends to congeal.) This first layer of polish will coat the entire surface of the water. Then drizzle on darker colors to create swirly shapes. Use a toothpick to combine colors organically. Work quickly; nail polish is designed to dry in minutes. When you're happy with your design, lightly dip the surface of your piece onto the polish and lift straight up. Pour in fresh polish for each subsequent piece you are going to paint. Let dry for at least 24 hours. Use the same technique on the slick surface of the drawer fronts as shown here.

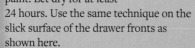

How to Marble

It's easy to master this technique for all the swirled projects on pages 26–28.

WHAT YOU'LL NEED

2 shallow glass or aluminum pans
   at least 2 inches larger than paper
   (do not use plastic)
alum (find it in the spice aisle at the
   grocery store)
water
blank paper (thick, uncoated paper
   works best)
iron
acrylic paint in at least two colors
liquid starch
toothpicks
tweezers
clothes hangers
clothespins

WHAT YOU DO

1. Gather materials as shown in Photo A. Add water 1 cup at a time in the pan to a depth of two inches. Mix in 1 tablespoon of alum per 1 cup of water as shown in Photo B.

2. Submerge paper in the alum solution. (Alternatively, you can use a paintbrush or sponge to paint the alum mixture onto paper.) Rinse lightly and let dry. Use an iron on the lowest heat setting to remove wrinkles from the paper.

3. Use water to dilute the acrylic paint by 50 percent. Repeat this process for all your colors. (Tip: Remove half of the paint from a paint squeeze bottle and replace it with water. This makes it easy to apply the paint in the next steps.)

4. In another pan add at least 2 inches of liquid starch. Test the weight of the paint by squeezing a tiny drop of diluted paint into the starch. If it sinks, dilute the paint further. If it floats, proceed to Step 5.

5. Squeeze diluted paint in a swirly, random pattern onto the surface of the starch as shown in Photo C. Add other colors; use a toothpick to swirl as shown in Photo D.

6. Gently place paper on the paint for 8 to 10 seconds as shown in Photo E. Carefully lift the paper by one edge from the water. If desired, use tweezers. Try not to shift the paper or remove it quickly as the pattern could smear.

7. Hang the paper from a hanger using clothespins as shown in Photo F. Dry for several hours.

Easy Does It
Happy Day

Bee Happy

Sure to make the celebrant smile, this bee gets its shape with subtle-pattern papers, crafting wire, and a few marking pen accents. Cut a 3½-inch circle from yellow paper for the body and 1½-inch head. Draw a face on the head and hot-glue a mini pom-pom as the nose. Cut a 3½-inch circle from black paper, cut to make three stripes as shown. Use a glue stick to adhere the stripes to body; glue body and head to a 5½×6-inch piece of white cardstock. Glue cardstock to a patterned piece of coordinating paper; trim a narrow border. Glue onto the front of a 6½×7-inch card. Cut or use a heart punch to make shape from dark pink; outline with marking pen dots. Use small pliers to shape wings, antennae, arms, and legs from wire. Use instant glue to secure pieces to card front and heart to bee's hands.

Pretty as a Rainbow

Your circle cutter makes this card a breeze to make. Cut circles in varying sizes from colored papers and glue together. Glue the circles to the front of a round note card. Tie a ribbon bow around a birthday candle and glue to the center of the circles.

Make a Wish

Send birthday wishes on the front of a card with baker's twine candles. Use the patterns on page 157 to cut candle and flame shapes from paper; then glue pieces of baker's twine to the front of the candles. Complete the card with sticker dots on the flames and a letter sticker greeting.

Banner Idea

These festive cards are so fun to make, you'll want to craft several at a time to have on hand. Use circle punches to cut 1- and 1½-inch circles from patterned paper; cut in half. Arrange the half-circles on a 4×8-inch piece of white cardstock as shown and tack in place with a tiny amount of glue stick near the rounded tips. Machine-stitch along the straight edges of the half-circles to create the look of mini banners. Write "celebrate" on a small strip of white cardstock, back with patterned paper, and trim a narrow border. Glue to card front. Layer the card top on patterned paper; cut a narrow border and then adhere to the front of a white 5×9-inch card

Sweet Surprise

Create a no-melt treat birthday card. Fold cardstock in half and use the pattern on page 158 to cut the shape. Use a crafts stick to smear hot glue along top edge of card front; sprinkle with beads and let dry. Glue 2 crafts sticks to back of card for handles.

Party On

Pick a metal animal head from the crafts store and cut a small paper hat to fit. Accordion-fold a 1×2-inch paper strip and wrap center with narrow strip secured with glue for bow. Hot-glue shapes to card front, detailing hat with pom-poms.

spring

BURSTING WITH COLOR

REFRESH

As the season unfolds, infuse your rooms with the fresh colors and symbolic motifs that make spring so beautiful.

Easter Cheer

Give your Easter table a color boost
with baskets, bunnies, eggs, and napkin rings cut
out of springtime patterned scrapbook papers.

Down the Bunny Trail

Silhouettes of bunnies and eggs add playful Easter touches. Trace patterns, page 156, onto tracing paper. Use patterns to cut shapes from print paper. Use glue stick to adhere shapes to white cardstock; trim narrow borders. To make them stand, cut slits where indicated and insert stand pieces. For sturdier stands, weight silhouettes by sawing slits in the center of wood blocks: 2-inch blocks for bunnies and 1-inch blocks for eggs.

Eggscellent Cover

Give plastic eggs a stylish makeover by hiding seams with colorful bands. Cut ½-inch-wide paper strips to fit around eggs, back with white cardstock, and glue layers together. Trim the edges with scallop-edge scissors. Wrap bands around filled plastic eggs and tape the ends to the egg.

Painted Tulip Flowerpot

Freshen a plain terra-cotta flowerpot with a coat of acrylic paint. When dry, lightly sand the edges.

Dainty Napkin Ring

A pleated napkin holds its folds with this pretty paper napkin ring. Cut a 2×8-inch strip from printed paper and glue to white cardstock. Trim a narrow border with scallop-edge scissors. Punch a hole in each end, ½ inch from the end. Thread with ribbon and tie into a bow.

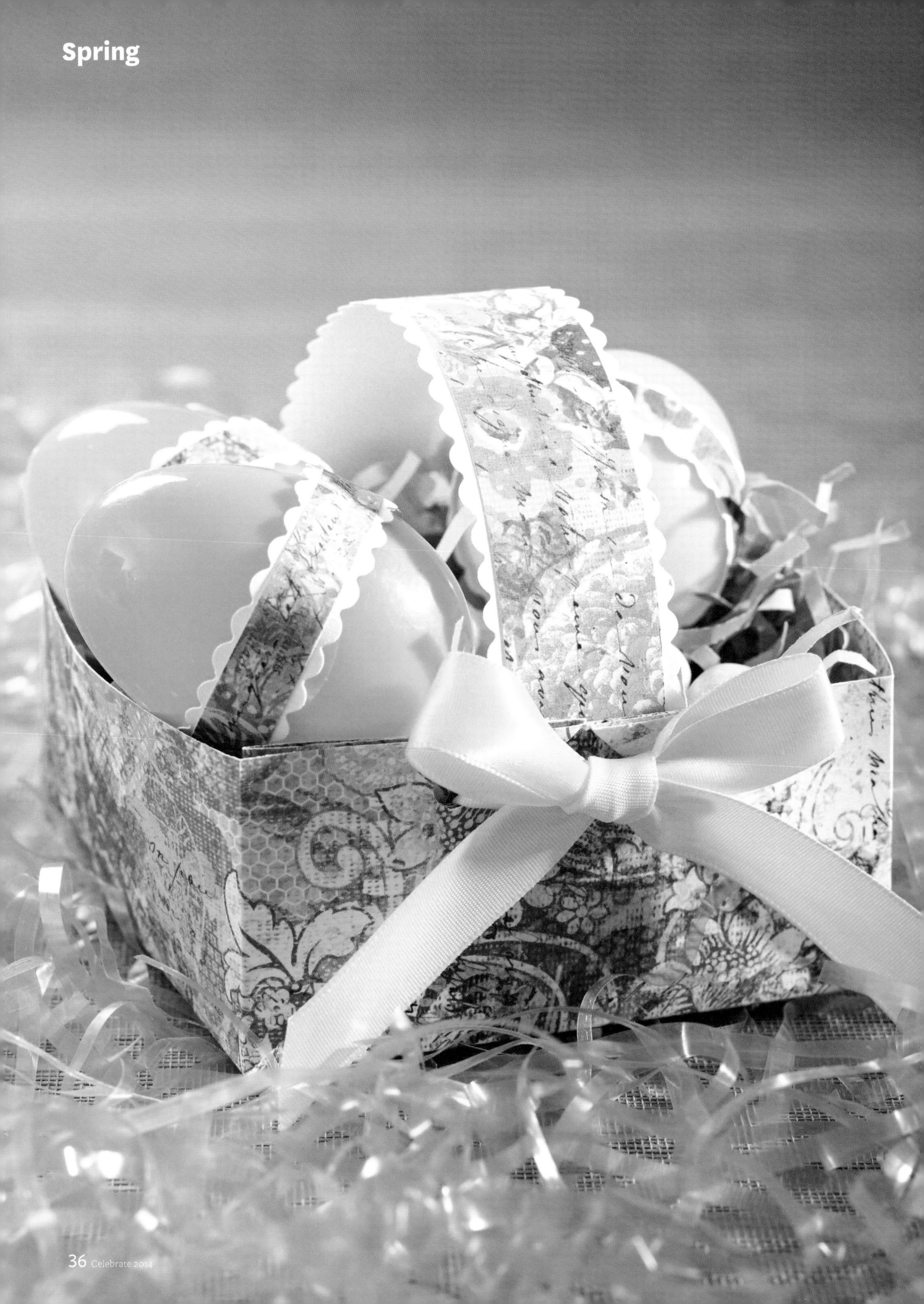

Beautiful Basket

Just the size for an Easter favor, these lightweight baskets fold easily from an 8-inch square of printed cardstock.

WHAT YOU'LL NEED

8-inch square and 1×8-inch strip of printed scrapbook
pencil
ruler
paper punch
½-inch-wide satin ribbon
2×8-inch strip of white cardstock
glue stick
scallop-edge scissors
hot-glue gun and glue sticks

WHAT YOU DO

1. Using a pencil and ruler, draw rules on the wrong side of the paper square, each 2 inches from the edge. In each corner, draw rules from the corner to the opposite corner as shown in Photo A.
2. Fold each edge toward center along fold line.
3. Fold corner triangles toward each other on each end as shown in Photo B.
4. Punch a hole through all layers on each end triangle as shown in Photo C.
5. Thread ribbon through holes on each end with tails to the outside of the basket bottom as shown in Photo D. Tie ends into a bow.

6. To make the handle, use glue stick to adhere printed rectangle to white cardstock. Trim white cardstock close to edge of printed paper to create a scalloped edge.
7. Slip each handle end under the ribbons on the inside of the basket and hot-glue in place.

Eggceptional

Hang on to those ribbon scraps—it doesn't take much to transform colored eggs into sensations.

From the Sewing Basket

Blanket wooden eggs with homespun charm. Paint each egg with acrylic paint in desired color; let dry. Use hot glue to adhere short lengths of ribbon, rickrack, lace, or other trim around egg center. On egg front (opposite of trim ends), glue on a button or two as the focal point.

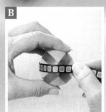

Beribboned Beauties

Here's another great way to use snippets of ribbon. Choose narrow ribbons to run vertically on egg (up to ½ inch wide) and ribbons up to 1 inch wide for horizontal pieces. Start with a narrow ribbon and glue the tail on the bottom of a wood egg as shown in Photo A. Wrap ribbon around the top of egg and glue end on egg bottom. Repeat with a second ribbon, positioning to make an "X" on egg top. Repeat with two more narrow ribbons, placing between secured ribbons as shown in Photo B. Place a dab of hot glue in center of egg as shown in Photo C. Adhere end of wide ribbon to glue. Weave ribbon in and out of narrow ribbons as shown in Photo D. Hot-glue ribbon end to egg.

Cool Patina

Pastels not in your Easter palette? Try this one-of-a-kind egg that has shabby chic written all over it.

WHAT YOU'LL NEED
fingernail polish in lime green and orange
paper towel
rub-on numbers and letters
round-ended paintbrush
wood wheels in 2½- and 1½-inch diameters
2-inch decorative spindle with tapered ends to fit wheels
black paint
burlap fabric or wide ribbon

WHAT YOU DO
1. Paint wood egg with green nail polish as shown in Photo A. Let the polish dry.
2. Using orange nail polish, paint random lines on the egg as shown in Photo B. Immediately dab off some of the orange polish to enhance the textural look as shown in Photo C. Let the polish dry.
3. Use the rounded end of a paintbrush to roughly burnish rub-on numbers and letters onto the egg surface as shown in Photo D, overlapping as desired. To enhance the worn vintage appeal, don't rub off all numbers and letters in their entirety.
4. To make the stand, use a 2½- and a 1½-inch wood wheel and a 2-inch decorative spindle with tapered ends to fit wheels as shown in Photo E. To paint on a textured background, hold a piece of burlap fabric or ribbon on one of the wheels. Paint through the holes with black paint as shown in Photo F, covering about half of the wheel. Repeat with the remaining wheel and spindle; let dry.
5. Press a wheel onto each end of the spindle to make the stand. If joints are loose, secure with hot glue.

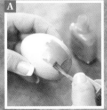
A

B

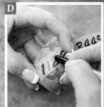
C

D

E

F

Vintage Appeal

Metal locks and keys—charms straight from the scrapbooking aisle in the crafts store—lend an unexpected feel of yesteryear to Easter eggs. To keep the egg monochromatic, wrap it with string. To secure the string end, hot-glue it near the bottom of the egg as shown in Photos A and B. Working in small sections, paint the egg with decoupage medium as shown in Photo C and wrap string over it as shown below until egg is covered. Hot-glue a charm to the egg and tie with a snippet of string or jute. Add a mini paper tag if desired.

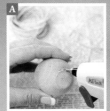

Lace Egg

Add a frilly surprise to Easter baskets. To make a lace egg, place it in the center of a piece of lace fabric large enough to cover it. Pull cut edges together to make lace taut to egg; secure with a rubber band. Holding lace "tails," dip egg in dye for approximately 30 seconds; pat dry. Clip rubber band, remove lace, and let dry.

Doodle Away

With a white ceramic egg as the canvas, you can create your own mini masterpiece. Use a medium-tip black permanent marking pen to doodle curlicue lines on one side of the egg as shown in Photo A, *opposite*. Broaden some of the strokes with marking pen as shown in Photo B. Use colored marking pens to color in various areas of design as shown in Photo C. Add a few marking-pen dots following the curvature of the lines as shown in Photo D.

Pretty Perch

A textured blue sky sets off a black bird silhouette with style. To create it, paint a small section of wood egg with decoupage medium as shown in Photo A. Stick crepe paper streamer to the decoupage medium and brush on top of the paper as shown in Photo B. Continue working in sections until entire egg is covered; let dry. Using very little paint on the brush, lightly brush over textured egg as shown in Photo C, allowing paint to cover raised areas of the paper; let dry.

No-Stitch Stitches

Give eggs a charm all their own with inspiration from the sewing basket. To make a dappled background, paint a wood egg with gold; dab with a crinkled paper towel to remove some of the paint and let dry. Hot-glue flower-shape buttons to one side, varying the placement as shown. Use half a snap for each flower center; hot-glue in place. Draw dotted-line stems to resemble running stitches and lazy-daisy leaves with a permanent marking pen.

Run for the Roses

Celebrate the granddaddy of all horse races using its slogan to inspire the decorating theme.

Showy Presentation

Flea-market sugar bowls in silver and gold tones make snazzy holders for race-day cupcakes. Serving the desserts in mismatched pieces adds to the fun of the day. Top each cupcake with a small rosebud, with the stem wrapped in cellophane.

Favored to Win

Premade muslin bags make great favors and offer a natural background to show off painted rose motifs. To simplify painting, make the rose prints using the bottom portion of celery. Wash and dry the celery. Cut off stalks, leaving bottom portion intact as shown in Photo A. Cut a piece of cardstock to fit inside the bag and slip it in as shown in Photo B. Use a paintbrush to spread yellow paint onto cut end of celery as shown in Photo C. Press painted end of celery onto bag as shown in Photo D. Wash off paint from celery, dry, and print. Print again with silver. Let dry. Hot-glue dimensional letters, the race initials or guest's names, onto front.

Just Rosie

Customize party invitations with the same celery-print technique. Start with a 4×6-inch piece of white cardstock. Print roses on the paper using yellow paint; let dry. Back the cardstock with gray paper using glue stick; trim a narrow border. Back again with yellow paper and trim a ½-inch border. Cut a ½×4¾-inch strip of white cardstock and write "you are invited" across it; leave ends free. Glue to gray and white polka-dot paper; trim a narrow border. Use brads to attach the strip to the front as shown. Adhere layers to the front of a 6×8-inch gray polka-dot card. Cut notched ends on a ¼-inch-wide piece of gray-print ribbon and a 1-inch-wide piece of yellow and white polka-dot ribbon. Use fabric glue to adhere the narrow ribbon atop the wider ribbon. Hot-glue ribbon to left of message strip, securing tails at top of card back.

Cinco de Mayo

Let the fiesta begin with a myriad of colorful ideas to
honor the culture of Mexico.

Gathering Place

Bursts of color against natural tones create an inviting atmosphere for a Cinco de Mayo get-together.

Colors in the Wind

Vivid flags, cut from bright tissue paper, add gentle movement as they catch the spring breeze. To make one, fold an 8½×22-inch sheet of tissue paper in half, short ends together. Fold a 4×10-inch piece of paper in half lengthwise. Slip the ends of the folded tissue paper into the paper sleeve as shown in Photo A. This helps the cutter make a clean cut on the tissue paper without ripping. Use a scallop border punch, such as in Photo B, to trim a decorative border. Fold the flag in half as shown in Photo C. Fold the flag again as shown in Photo D. Fold one more time to create a triangle as shown in Photo E. Use scissors to cut designs in the folded tissue paper as you would a snowflake as shown in Photos F and G. Be sure not to cut too much of the paper away or to make cuts too intricate. Unfold and iron carefully with a press cloth. Hang over a rope, stapling at the top to create a casing. Slip a wood bead between each paper flag for added detail.

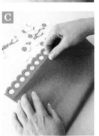

Button Up

Keep it casual with napkin rings made of oversize buttons strung on lengths of natural jute. Look for those that slide right into your festive color palette. Tuck in sprigs of fresh flowers to add meaningful touches to the celebration.

Fresh Picked

Send guests home with a mini nosegay of fresh flowers. To keep stems together, thread through a large wood bead. To keep blooms healthy, poke stems into a floral water tube.

Candy Cup

Elegant in its presentation but super simple to achieve, this serving trick uses a decorative cupcake liner. Place it in a margarita glass before filling with candy for a totally polished look.

Too-Cute Ties

Jute threaded with large wood beads gives stemmed glasses instant appeal. Use smaller beads at the ends to help prevent beads slipping over the knots at the ends. If you want to use these colorful add-ons as glass tags, fashion each one using just one or two colors of beads for each glass so guests can tell their drinks apart.

Table Trinkets

Welcome large cacti to the table by placing them in colorful plastic containers. Group them together to make their presence more prominent.

Take Me Home
Guests will thank you again and again for these mini succulent favors. Line a plastic margarita glass with a couple squares of colored tissue paper and place a mini planter into the center. Tie a beaded piece of jute around the stem for a fun party token.

A Vase for Mom

Moms love flowers on their day of honor,
and these vases add an endearing personal touch.

Simply Beautiful

A coat of latex paint on the inside of a glass vase, followed by a scale pattern drawn on the outside with a paint pen, takes a vase from plain to pretty. A plastic insert helps preserve the interior paint.

Get Centered

Craft a vase in no time by wrapping a wood or glass vase in wallpaper. Measure the container's dimensions, adding 1 inch to the circumference for overlap. Cut the paper to fit and affix with spray adhesive. If the vase is glass, add water and flowers. If it's wood, set the blooms inside a jar or cup before placing them in the vase.

Boldly Folded

Handcrafted vase wraps ensconce simple blooms.

WHAT YOU'LL NEED
straightedge or ruler
pencil
2-ply vellum-finish
    paper
bone folder
cutting mat

WHAT YOU DO
1. Use a straightedge and pencil to mark on the paper vertical lines spaced 1 inch apart.
2. Mark a straight diagonal line from corner to corner, both ways, so that in addition to vertical lines, you have a large "X." Make additional diagonal lines spaced 1½ inches apart as shown in Photo A.
3. Using a bone folder, score the vertical lines. Make valley folds at the vertical lines as shown in Photo B. A valley fold is formed by folding the sides of the paper upward so that each fold line creates a V-shape valley.
4. Score the diagonal lines and make mountain folds. A mountain fold is created by folding the sides downward.
5. Wrap the paper around a glass jar and attach with glue at the seam in the back. To vary the look, experiment with the spacing between mountain and valley folds.

Cute Boot

Short on time? Line a patterned rain boot with a jar and tuck Mom's favorite blooms inside. Wrap up the other boot in a gift box and Mom has a pair to wear when the raindrops fall.

Backyard Retreat

Fresh and cheery, gingham patterns launch an outdoor get-together beautifully.

Sail Away

Talk about favors that float your boat! Rectangular favor cups form bases for these sailboat treat caddies. Fold a 4-inch paper square in half diagonally to make sail. Secure points with a single cross-stitch. Trim a small notch out of the fold, approximately 3 inches from bottom point of fold. Hot-glue a 6-inch-long lollipop stick in the center bottom of the cup. Insert lollipop stick through hole in sail. Personalize with alphabet stickers. Fill boat with desired snack mix, nuts, or candy.

Good Service
Collanders make fun serving vessels, and you don't have to worry about breakage. Line with a paper napkin if desired and use them to hold fruit, chips, candy—anything that won't seep through the drainage holes.

Plate Pizzazz

Paper plates with any check pattern make it easy to add a few cross-stitches to the border. Place a piece of plastic foam behind the plate and use a safety pin to poke holes in the corners of the squares where stitches are desired. Using embroidery floss and a needle, sew cross-stitches on the plate rim, away from food area.

Winged Wiper

A paper napkin transforms quickly into a fluttery butterfly. Accordion-pleat the napkin and secure it in the middle with a chenille stem. Shape the tails into antennae.

Center of Attention

Decorate the centerpiece in the gingham theme. Trim the top of a sprinkling can with strips of gingham paper or layers of ribbon; tape in place. Tie a gingham ribbon bow to the top of the handle. Use the can to hold a colorful spring bouquet.

Easy Does It
Recycle Blast

Seeing Spots

Use bottle caps to add texture, color, and playful pattern to a plain table. Spray-paint both sides of the caps with primer; let dry. Divide caps and spray-paint each group the desired color; let dry. Use contact cement to attach caps to the tabletop. For extra protection and a smooth surface, top the bottle caps with a piece of tempered glass cut to the size of the tabletop.

Monogram Map

Rescue outdated maps from hitting the trash by commemorating special destinations with map-covered papier-mâché letters. Trace around a letter onto map paper and cut out. Use decoupage medium to adhere the cutout to the letter front. Let dry and add a second coat for durability. Let medium dry before adding flag-top pins to mark favorite cities.

Put a Cork in It

Raise your glass with a coaster that does it for you. Start with a coaster-size shadowbox. Fill it snuggly with wine corks and hot-glue them in place. To protect from table scratches, place an adhesive rubber bumpers on the bottom corners.

Pop Art

Refresh your message center with a magnetic bottle-cap board. Use new or vintage bottle caps arranged into a heart shape and glued onto a pattern-paper-covered frame backing. Use additional magnet-backed bottle caps to attach notes on the display.

Can Do

Labels removed, tin cans provide naturally watertight vessels to hold favorite seasonal picks. Group several can sizes together to make a stunning centerpiece display.

Made to Measure

Chalk up this idea to a salvaged contractor's ruler. Cut a board to fit the back of the folded-ruler frame, coat with chalkboard paint, and screw it onto the back of the ruler frame. The thick frame makes the perfect chalk ledge.

CHICKEN BREAST
PAILLARD WITH
GRILLED ROMAINE
page 79

food

TASTE THE FUN

Good food is at the center of any gathering with family and friends, whatever the time of year. Cook up a special occasion with these recipes for good times, from a St. Patrick's Day feast to a fondue party perfect for celebrating a beautiful fall day.

GRILLED CORN COB BITES
WITH CHILE AND LIME,
page 76

An Irish Feast

This March 17, invite friends over for the wearing of the green, the raising of a glass, feasting on a tasty St. Patrick's Day spread—and a bit of blarney, too!

CORNED BEEF AND CABBAGE, page 66

CURRANT-ORANGE IRISH SODA BREAD,
page 66

Corned Beef and Cabbage

Although this dish was not created in Ireland, it was created by Irish immigrants in this country and has become required eating on St. Patrick's Day.

PREP 15 minutes SLOW COOK 10 hours (low) or 5 hours (high)

WHAT YOU NEED
1   3-pound corned beef brisket with spice packet
½   of a small head cabbage, cut into 3 wedges
4   medium carrots, halved lengthwise and cut into 2-inch pieces
2   medium Yukon gold or yellow Finn potatoes, cut into 2-inch pieces
1   medium onion, quartered
½   cup water

WHAT YOU DO
1. Trim fat from meat. If necessary, cut meat to fit into a 5- to 6-quart slow cooker. Sprinkle spices from packet evenly over meat; rub in with your fingers. Place cabbage, carrots, potatoes, and onion in cooker. Add the water. Place meat on top of vegetables.
2. Cover and cook on low for 10 to 12 hours or on high for 5 to 6 hours.
3. Transfer meat to a serving platter; thinly slice across the grain. Using a slotted spoon, transfer vegetables to a serving platter. Makes 6 servings.

Currant-Orange Irish Soda Bread

Thick slices of this currant-studded bread are best served warm, slathered with butter.

PREP 20 minutes BAKE 30 minutes OVEN 375°F

WHAT YOU NEED
2   cups all-purpose flour
1   to 2 tablespoons sugar
1   teaspoon baking powder
½   teaspoon baking soda
½   teaspoon salt
1   tablespoon finely shredded orange peel
3   tablespoons butter
⅓   cup currants
1   egg, lightly beaten
¾   cup buttermilk

WHAT YOU DO
1. Preheat oven to 375°F. Grease a baking sheet; set aside. In a large mixing bowl stir together flour, sugar, baking powder, baking soda, salt, and orange peel. Cut in butter until mixture resembles coarse crumbs. Stir in currants. Make a well in the center of the mixture.
2. In a small mixing bowl combine egg and buttermilk. Add all at once to flour mixture. Stir just until moistened.
3. On a lightly floured surface gently knead dough to form a dough (about 4 or 5 times). Shape into a 7-inch round loaf.
4. Transfer dough to prepared baking sheet. With a sharp knife, make two slashes across the top of the loaf to form an X, cutting all the way to the edge. Bake 30 to 35 minutes or until golden. Serve warm. Makes 12 servings.

Shamrock Milkshake Cupcakes

Tender buttermilk white-cake cupcakes are flavored and tinted with crème de menthe liqueur and topped with white chocolate frosting in the shape of a four-leaf clover in these St. Paddy's Day treats.

PREP 50 minutes
STAND 30 minutes BAKE 15 minutes
OVEN 350°F
COOL 45 minutes

WHAT YOU NEED
4   egg whites
2   cups all-purpose flour
1   teaspoon baking powder
½   teaspoon baking soda
½   teaspoon salt
1   cup buttermilk or sour milk*
¼   cup green crème de menthe**
½   cup shortening
1¾ cups sugar
1   teaspoon vanilla
1   recipe White Chocolate Frosting (see recipe, right)
    Green food coloring

WHAT YOU DO
1. Allow egg whites to stand at room temperature for 30 minutes. Meanwhile, line twenty to twenty-two 2½-inch muffin cups with paper bake cups. In a medium bowl stir together flour, baking powder, baking soda, and salt. In a 2-cup glass measuring cup combine buttermilk and crème de menthe. Set aside.
2. Preheat oven to 350°F. In a large mixing bowl beat shortening with an electric mixer on medium to high speed for 30 seconds. Gradually add sugar, about ¼ cup at a time, beating on medium speed until light and fluffy. Beat in vanilla. Add egg whites, one at a time, beating well after each addition. Alternately add flour mixture and buttermilk mixture to shortening mixture, beating on low speed after each addition just until mixture is combined.
3. Spoon batter into prepared muffin cups, filling each about two-thirds full. Use the back of a spoon to smooth out batter in cups.
4. Bake for 15 to 18 minutes or until tops spring back when lightly touched. Cool cupcakes in muffin cups on wire racks for 5 minutes. Remove cupcakes from muffin cups. Cool completely on wire racks.
5. Divide White Chocolate Frosting between two bowls. Tint one portion with green food coloring. Spoon each frosting into a pastry bag fitted with a large star tip. Pipe white and green frostings onto tops of cupcakes to resemble four-leaf clovers. Makes 20 to 22 (2½-inch) cupcakes.
*TIP: For each 1 cup sour milk, place 1 tablespoon lemon juice or vinegar in a glass measuring cup. Add enough milk to make 1 cup total liquid; stir. Let stand for 5 minutes before using.
**TIP: If you prefer not to use crème de menthe, substitute a mixture of ¼ cup milk, 1 teaspoon mint extract, and several drops green food coloring.
White Chocolate Frosting: Place 6 ounces chopped white baking chocolate in a large mixing bowl; set aside. In a small saucepan heat ⅓ cup whipping cream just until simmering. Pour over white baking chocolate; let stand, without stirring, for 5 minutes. Stir until smooth; let stand for 15 minutes. Gradually beat 1 cup softened butter into melted white chocolate mixture with an electric mixer on medium to high speed, beating until combined. Gradually beat in 1½ to 2 cups powdered sugar until frosting reaches piping or spreading consistency. Makes 3½ cups.

"**For each petal on the shamrock,** this brings a wish your way. Good health, good luck, and happiness for today and every day." —IRISH BLESSING

SHAMROCK MILKSHAKE CUPCAKES

Cinco de Mayo

The 5th of May is the day to celebrate all things Mexican—the music, the culture, the dancing— and especially the food and drink!

CLASSIC MARGARITAS, page 70

GRILLED CHICKEN
FINGER FAJITAS
WITH PEPPERS AND
ONIONS, page 70

Classic Margaritas

Margaritas made fresh stand head and shoulders above the prepared versions—and they couldn't be simpler to make.

START TO FINISH **15 minutes**

WHAT YOU NEED

- 3 cups Triple Sec or other orange liqueur
- 2 to 3 cups tequila
- 1½ cups freshly squeezed lime juice
- 1 cup superfine sugar or powdered sugar
  Kosher salt
- 9 lime wedges
  Ice cubes

WHAT YOU DO

1. In a pitcher combine Triple Sec, tequila, fresh lime juice, and sugar. Stir until sugar is dissolved. Chill the mixture until ready to serve.

2. Place salt on a small plate. Rub rims of 8 glasses with one of the lime wedges. Dip rims of glasses in salt to coat.

3. Place ice cubes in salt-rimmed glasses. Pour tequila mixture over ice cubes. Garnish with remaining lime wedges. Makes 8 servings.

Grilled Chicken Finger Fajitas with Peppers and Onions

This is perfect party food—interactive and completely customizable—because guests make their own fajita to order.

PREP **15 minutes** GRILL **20 minutes**

WHAT YOU NEED

- ½ cup Mexican crema or sour cream
- 2 teaspoons taco seasoning or Mexican seasoning blend
- 1 pound chicken breast tenderloins
- 2 tablespoons fajita seasoning blend
- 2 tablespoons olive oil
- 2 tablespoons lime juice
- 1 tablespoon bottled hot sauce
- 1 fresh poblano pepper, stemmed, quartered lengthwise, and seeded*
- 1 red sweet pepper, stemmed, quartered lengthwise, and seeded
- 1 onion, peeled and cut crosswise into ⅓-inch-thick rings
  Olive oil
  Salt
- 8 6- to 7-inch flour tortillas
  Guacamole
  Shredded cheese
  Salsa or pico de gallo

WHAT YOU DO

1. In a small bowl stir together the crema and taco seasoning; set aside.

2. In a large bowl combine the chicken tenderloins, fajita seasoning, olive oil, lime juice, and hot sauce; toss until well coated. Set aside.

3. Brush poblano, red sweet pepper, and onion pieces with oil; season with salt. Grill the vegetables on the rack of a covered grill directly over medium heat for 8 to 10 minutes or until vegetables are tender and slightly charred, turning occasionally. Remove from grill.

4. Add chicken to grill. Cover and grill for 4 to 5 minutes or until no longer pink, turning once. Transfer to a platter.

5. Add the tortillas to the grill. Grill for 20 to 30 seconds per side or until tortillas are heated through.

6. Chop vegetables into bite-size pieces and place in a serving bowl. Serve chicken with crema, vegetables, tortillas, guacamole, cheese, and salsa. Makes 4 servings.

*TIP: Because chile peppers contain volatile oils that can burn your skin and eyes, avoid direct contact with them as much as possible. When working with chile peppers, wear plastic or rubber gloves. If your bare hands do touch the peppers, wash your hands and nails well with soap and warm water.

Chunky Guacamole

Serve this textured guacamole with sturdy tortilla chips as a munchie with Classic Margaritas while the fajitas are on the grill.

START TO FINISH **20 minutes**

WHAT YOU NEED

- 2 roma tomatoes, seeded and finely chopped (⅔ cup)
- 2 green onions, sliced (¼ cup)
- 2 tablespoons lime juice
- 1 tablespoon olive oil
- 1 to 2 cloves garlic, minced
- ¼ teaspoon salt
- ⅛ teaspoon ground black pepper
- 2 very ripe avocados, halved, seeded, peeled, and coarsely mashed

WHAT YOU DO

1. In a medium bowl combine tomatoes, green onions, lime juice, oil, garlic, salt, and pepper. Gently stir in avocados. Serve immediately or cover the surface with plastic wrap and chill for up to 1 hour. Makes 16 servings.

CHUNKY GUACAMOLE

Refried Beans

PREP 20 minutes STAND 1 hour
COOK 2 hours 38 minutes

WHAT YOU NEED
- 8 ounces dried pinto beans (about 1¼ cups)
- 8 cups water
- ½ teaspoon salt
- 2 tablespoons bacon drippings or olive oil
- 2 cloves garlic, minced
  Queso fresco (optional)

WHAT YOU DO
1. Rinse beans. In a large saucepan or Dutch oven combine beans and 4 cups of the water. Bring to boiling; reduce heat. Simmer, covered, for 2 minutes. Remove from heat. Cover and let stand for 1 hour. (Or place beans in water in pan. Cover and let soak in a cool place overnight.) Drain and rinse beans.
2. In the same pan combine beans, 4 cups fresh water, and the salt. Bring to boiling; reduce heat. Simmer, covered, for 2½ to 3 hours or until beans are very tender. Drain beans, reserving liquid.
3. In a heavy large skillet heat bacon drippings. Stir in garlic. Add beans; mash thoroughly with a potato masher. Stir in enough of the cooking liquid (about ¼ cup) to make a pastelike mixture. Cook, uncovered, over low heat for 8 to 10 minutes or until mixture is thick, stirring often. Sprinkled with crumbled queso fresco if desired. Makes 4 servings.

Mexican Red Rice

PREP 20 minutes COOK 23 minutes
STAND 5 minutes

WHAT YOU NEED
- 1 tablespoon vegetable oil
- ½ cup chopped onion (1 medium)
- 2 cloves garlic, minced
- 1 teaspoon ground ancho chile pepper
- ¼ teaspoon kosher salt
- 1 cup long grain rice
- 1 14.5-ounce can reduced-sodium chicken broth or vegetable broth
- ¾ cup Roasted Salsa Roja (see recipe, right) or purchased salsa
- ¼ cup water
- ½ cup finely snipped fresh cilantro

WHAT YOU DO
1. In a medium saucepan heat oil over medium-high heat. Add onion, garlic, ground ancho chile pepper, and salt; cook for 2 minutes. Stir in uncooked rice; cook

REFRIED BEANS AND MEXICAN RED RICE

and stir for 1 minute. Add broth, Roasted Salsa Roja, and the water. Bring to boiling; reduce heat. Simmer, covered, about 20 minutes or until rice is tender.
2. Remove pan from heat. Remove lid. Cover pan with a clean kitchen towel; replace lid. Let stand for 5 minutes to let the towel absorb any excess moisture. Remove lid and towel. Add cilantro; fluff rice with a fork. Makes 6 servings.

Roasted Salsa Roja

PREP 30 minutes BROIL 14 minutes
COOL 10 minutes

WHAT YOU NEED
- 3 medium tomatoes (about 1½ pounds total), quartered and cored
- 1 small onion, quartered
- 5 cloves garlic, peeled
- 1 fresh jalapeño chile pepper, halved and seeded*
- 2 to 3 tablespoons vegetable oil
- 1 cup fresh cilantro leaves, snipped
- ¼ to ⅓ cup lime juice
- ½ teaspoon sugar
- 1 teaspoon salt

WHAT YOU DO
1. Preheat broiler. In a large bowl combine tomatoes, onion, garlic, and chile pepper; toss with just enough of the oil to coat. Spoon into a 15×10×1-inch baking pan, spreading evenly.
2. Broil 5 to 6 inches from heat for 8 minutes. Turn vegetables. Broil for 6 to 8 minutes more or until edges begin to darken. Transfer baking pan to a wire rack; cool for 10 minutes.

3. Transfer roasted vegetables and their cooking juices to a food processor; pulse until coarsely chopped. Add cilantro, lime juice, and sugar; pulse until salsa is desired consistency. Season to taste with salt. Serve immediately or cover and chill. Makes 3 cups.

*TIP: Because chile peppers contain volatile oils that can burn your skin and eyes, avoid direct contact with them as much as possible. When working with chile peppers, wear plastic or rubber gloves. If your bare hands do touch the peppers, wash your hands and nails well with soap and warm water.

Salsa Fresca Variation: Prepare as directed, except coarsely chop all the vegetables, omit the oil, and omit Steps 1 and 2. Process in food processor as directed in Step 3.

Mocha Tres Leches Cake

PREP 40 minutes BAKE 30 minutes
COOL 1 hour 25 minutes CHILL 3 hours
OVEN 325°F

WHAT YOU NEED

6   eggs
¾   cup milk
¾   cup unsweetened cocoa powder
1¾ cups all-purpose flour
4   teaspoons baking powder
1   teaspoon salt
1½ cups granulated sugar
2   teaspoons vanilla
1   12-ounce can evaporated milk
3   tablespoons instant espresso
     coffee powder
1   14-ounce can sweetened
     condensed milk
¾   cup whipping cream
½   of an 8-ounce package cream
     cheese, softened
1   cup powdered sugar
1½ cups whipping cream
     Chocolate jimmies (optional)

WHAT YOU DO

1. Preheat oven to 325°F. Separate eggs, placing egg whites in a very large bowl and yolks in a small bowl; set aside. In a small saucepan heat the ¾ cup milk over medium heat until simmering; remove from heat. Whisk in the cocoa powder (mixture will be thick); set aside to cool.
2. In a small bowl combine the flour and baking powder; set aside. Beat the egg whites and salt with an electric mixer on medium speed until frothy. Increase

speed to medium-high and beat until soft peaks form (tips curl). Slowly add the granulated sugar, beating mixture until stiff peaks form.
3. Add egg yolks to the beaten whites and beat just until combined. Add the flour and cooled chocolate mixture alternately to the egg mixture, beating well after each addition. Add the vanilla and beat just until combined.
4. Pour batter into an ungreased 13×9×2-inch baking pan, spreading evenly. Bake for 30 to 35 minutes or until a toothpick inserted near the center comes out clean. Transfer cake to a cooling rack and cool completely in the pan (about 1 hour).
5. In a medium saucepan combine the evaporated milk and espresso powder. Heat over medium heat, stirring constantly, until the espresso powder has

dissolved. Remove from heat. Stir in the sweetened condensed milk and the ¾ cup whipping cream.
6. Use the tines of a long fork or a wooden skewer to poke holes all over the top of the cake. Pour the espresso mixture evenly over the top of the cake.
7. Meanwhile, in a medium bowl beat the cream cheese with an electric mixer on medium speed until smooth; beat in powdered sugar. Add ¼ cup of the whipping cream and beat until combined. Add remaining whipping cream and beat until soft peaks form.
8. Pipe or spread whipped cream mixture over cake and refrigerate for 3 to 24 hours, covering cake after topper is set. If desired, sprinkle with chocolate jimmies. Makes 16 servings.

Garden-Fresh Grilling

When gardens and farmer's markets burst with summer bounty, host a backyard barbecue to celebrate the best, freshest produce of the year—tart cherries, sweet corn, crisp lettuces, juicy peaches, and perfectly ripe berries.

PEPPERCORN-BLUE CHEESE
BURGERS WITH TANGY
CHERRY COMPOTE, page 76

GRILLED CORN COB BITES
WITH CHILE AND LIME,
page 76

Peppercorn-Blue Cheese Burgers with Tangy Cherry Compote

PREP 30 minutes COOK 20 minutes
GRILL 11 minutes

WHAT YOU NEED
1   pound pitted fresh or frozen tart cherries, thawed and drained (3 cups)
⅓   cup sugar
¼   cup dried cherries
2   tablespoons red wine vinegar
1   teaspoon snipped fresh rosemary
1¼ pounds ground beef chuck
½   teaspoon kosher salt
2   tablespoons coarsely cracked black peppercorns
6   ounces blue cheese, such as Gorgonzola dolce
6   hamburger buns, split

WHAT YOU DO
1. For the Tangy Cherry Compote, in a medium saucepan combine cherries, sugar, dried cherries, red wine vinegar, and rosemary. Bring to boiling over medium-high heat, stirring frequently. Reduce heat. Boil gently, uncovered, 20 minutes until thickened. Keep warm.
2. In a medium bowl season beef with salt. Shape beef into six ¾-inch-thick patties. Spread cracked peppercorns on plate; press one side of each patty into cracked pepper.
3. For a charcoal or gas grill, place patties on the grill rack directly over medium heat. Cover and grill for 10 to 12 minutes or until done (160°F), turning once halfway through grilling. Spread patties with blue cheese; let stand 5 minutes to melt cheese. Place buns, cut sides down, on grill rack for 1 to 2 minutes or until lightly toasted. Remove patties and buns from the grill.
4. Serve patties on buns with Tangy Cherry Compote. Pass remaining compote. Makes 6 servings.

Grilled Corn Cob Bites with Chile and Lime

There is actually a way to make summer sweet corn even better—and this is it: Grill and baste the ears with a lime-infused butter-sour cream-mayo mixture, then sprinkle with smoky Mexican-style seasoning right before serving.

PREP 20 minutes SOAK 10 minutes
GRILL 15 minutes

WHAT YOU NEED
6   large ears of corn, husks and silks removed
½   cup snipped fresh cilantro
1   tablespoon ground ancho chile pepper
2   teaspoons finely shredded lime peel
¼   to ½ teaspoon cayenne pepper
¼   cup butter, melted
2   tablespoons mayonnaise or salad dressing
2   tablespoons Mexican crema or sour cream
2   tablespoons lime juice
    Salt

WHAT YOU DO
1. Cut each ear of corn into thirds. Place corn pieces in a large pot and cover with water. Let soak for 10 minutes.
2. In a small bowl stir together cilantro, ground ancho chile pepper, lime peel, and cayenne pepper; set aside.
3. In an extra-large bowl whisk together butter, mayonnaise, crema, and lime juice; set aside. Drain corn. For a charcoal or gas grill, place corn on a grill directly over medium-high heat. Cover and grill for 15 to 20 minutes or until corn is tender, turning pieces every 5 minutes and brushing them with the butter mixture several times during the last 5 minutes of grilling.
4. Place grilled corn in the remaining butter mixture in the bowl; toss to coat. Sprinkle cilantro mixture over corn; toss to coat. Season to taste with salt. Makes 6 servings.

Sparkling Golden Sangria

For a nonalcoholic version of this refreshing summer sipper, see the variation below.

PREP 20 minutes CHILL 1 hour

WHAT YOU NEED
3   cups white grape juice, chilled
½   cup orange liqueur, such as Cointreau
¼   cup superfine or granulated sugar
3   tablespoons honey
1   medium nectarine, pitted and chopped
1   navel orange, quartered and thinly sliced
¾   cup fresh or frozen sweet cherries, pitted and halved, or canned mandarin orange sections, drained
¾   cup fresh golden or red raspberries
½   cup fresh basil leaves
½   cup fresh mint leaves
1   750-milliliter bottle sparkling white wine, chilled
    Ice

WHAT YOU DO
1. In a large pitcher or glass jar combine grape juice, orange liqueur, sugar, and honey, stirring until sugar and honey dissolve. Stir in nectarine, orange, cherries, raspberries, basil, and mint. Chill mixture for 1 hour or up to 24 hours, stirring occasionally.
2. To serve, add sparkling wine to fruit mixture. Serve in glasses over ice. Makes 8 servings.

Nonalcoholic Sparkling Sangria: Prepare as directed, except substitute orange juice for the orange liqueur and sparkling water or club soda for the sparkling white wine.

Easy living—and entertaining—in the summertime means gathering with friends on the patio or deck for breezy outdoor cooking and dining.

SPARKLING GOLDEN SANGRIA

CHICKEN BREAST
PAILLARD WITH
GRILLED ROMAINE

Chicken Breast Paillard with Grilled Romaine

A paillard is simply a thin, quick-cooking piece of meat or poultry.

PREP 25 minutes MARINATE 30 minutes GRILL 5 minutes

WHAT YOU NEED
¼ cup lemon juice
1 tablespoon minced shallots
1 tablespoon Dijon mustard
¼ teaspoon sugar
¼ teaspoon salt
½ cup olive oil
¼ cup finely chopped red sweet pepper
1 tablespoon snipped fresh tarragon
4 skinless, boneless chicken breast halves (6 to 7 ounces each)
2 hearts romaine lettuce, halved lengthwise
    Nonstick cooking spray
    Salt
    Ground black pepper
    Shaved Parmesan cheese

WHAT YOU DO
1. For the vinaigrette, in a medium bowl whisk together lemon juice, shallots, mustard, sugar, and the ¼ teaspoon salt. Gradually add olive oil, whisking until combined. Stir in sweet pepper and tarragon; cover and set aside.
2. For the chicken, place each chicken breast half between two pieces of plastic wrap. Using the flat side of a meat mallet, pound chicken lightly until ¼-inch thickness. Discard plastic wrap. Place chicken in a large resealable plastic bag set in a shallow dish. Add half of the vinaigrette. Seal bag; turn to coat chicken. Marinate in the refrigerator for 30 minutes to 3 hours.
3. Drain chicken, discarding marinade. For a charcoal grill, grill chicken on the greased rack of an uncovered grill directly over medium coals for 3 to 4 minutes or until no longer pink, turning once halfway through grilling. Lightly coat cut side of each romaine piece with cooking spray; sprinkle with salt and black pepper. Grill romaine, cut sides down, about 2 minutes or until edges char. (For a gas grill, preheat grill. Reduce heat to medium. Place chicken, and later romaine, on grill rack over heat. Cover and grill as above.)
4. To serve, place chicken and romaine, cut sides up, on four serving plates. Sprinkle with shaved Parmesan.

GRILLED ASPARAGUS WITH PARMESAN CURLS

Grilled Asparagus with Parmesan Curls

PREP 15 minutes MARINATE 30 minutes GRILL 3 minutes

WHAT YOU NEED
1½ pounds asparagus spears, trimmed
2 tablespoons olive oil
½ teaspoon finely shredded lemon peel (set aside)
2 tablespoons lemon juice
½ teaspoon salt
¼ teaspoon freshly ground black pepper
1 ounce Parmesan cheese or Manchego cheese
    Freshly ground black pepper (optional)

WHAT YOU DO
1. In a covered large skillet cook asparagus in a small amount of boiling water for 3 minutes; drain. Meanwhile, for marinade, in a 2-quart rectangular baking dish combine oil, lemon juice, salt, and the ¼ teaspoon pepper. Add asparagus, stirring to coat. Cover and marinate at room temperature for 30 minutes. Drain asparagus, discarding marinade. Place asparagus on a grill tray or in a grill basket.
2. For a charcoal grill, place asparagus on the rack of an uncovered grill directly over medium coals. Grill for 3 to 5 minutes or until asparagus is tender and starting to brown, turning once halfway through grilling. (For a gas grill, preheat grill. Reduce heat to medium. Place asparagus on grill rack over heat. Cover and grill as above.)
3. Arrange asparagus on a serving platter. Working over asparagus, use a cheese plane or vegetable peeler to cut thin, wide strips from the side of cheese block. Sprinkle asparagus with lemon peel and, if desired, additional pepper. Makes 6 servings.

GINGER PEACH MARGARITAS

Cast-Iron Mixed Berry Crisp

A topping of crushed Italian macaroons mixed with butter, brown sugar, and almonds crowns this homey crisp.

PREP 25 minutes STAND 15 minutes
GRILL 35 minutes COOL 30 minutes

WHAT YOU NEED
3 cups mixed fresh berries (such as blueberries, blackberries, and/or raspberries)
⅓ cup granulated sugar
4 teaspoons quick-cooking tapioca
½ teaspoon ground cinnamon
½ teaspoon ground ginger
½ cup crushed amaretti cookies
¼ cup all-purpose flour
2 tablespoons sliced almonds
2 tablespoons packed brown sugar
¼ cup butter
1 tablespoon butter, softened
Vanilla ice cream (optional)

WHAT YOU DO
1. In a large bowl combine berries, granulated sugar, tapioca, cinnamon, and ginger. Let stand for 15 minutes, stirring occasionally.
2. For the topping, in a medium bowl combine crushed amaretti, flour, almonds, and brown sugar. Using a pastry blender, cut in the ¼ cup butter until mixture resembles coarse crumbs.
3. Generously butter an 8- or 9-inch cast-iron skillet or two individual 10- to 12-ounce cast-iron skillets with the 1 tablespoon softened butter. Fill skillet(s) with berry mixture. Sprinkle with the topping.
4. For a charcoal grill, arrange medium-hot coals around the edges of the grill, leaving center of grill with no coals. Test for medium heat above the center of the grill. Place skillet(s) in center of grill rack (not over the coals). Cover and grill until bubbly and topping is golden brown. Allow about 35 minutes for large skillet or about 20 minutes for small skillets. (For a gas grill, preheat grill. Adjust for indirect cooking. Place skillet[s] on unheated side of grill. Grill as above.)
5. Remove from grill; let cool for 30 minutes before serving. If desired, serve warm with ice cream. Makes 4 servings.

Ginger Peach Margaritas
START TO FINISH 25 minutes

WHAT YOU NEED
1 tablespoon coarse sugar
1 tablespoon crystallized ginger, very finely chopped
1 lime
2 medium fresh peaches (6 to 8 ounces each), unpeeled, pitted, and cut up
1 recipe Ginger Syrup
½ cup tequila
⅓ cup Cointreau or Triple Sec
⅓ cup lime juice
2½ cups ice

WHAT YOU DO
1. In a shallow dish combine the sugar and crystallized ginger; set aside. Cut a thick slice of lime; cut slice in half. Rub halves around rims of 5 or 6 glasses. Dip rims into the sugar mixture to coat; set glasses aside. Slice remaining lime into 5 or 6 slices; set aside for garnish.
2. In a blender combine peaches, Ginger Syrup, tequila, Cointreau, and lime juice. Cover and blend until smooth. Gradually add ice cubes, blending until smooth (blender will be full). Pour into glasses. Garnish with the reserved lime slices. Makes 5 or 6 servings.
Ginger Syrup: In a small saucepan combine ¼ cup sugar, ¼ cup water, and one 1-inch piece fresh ginger, cut into thin slices. Bring to boiling, stirring constantly until the sugar is dissolved. Boil gently, uncovered, for 4 minutes or until thickened. Remove from heat; let cool. Remove and discard the ginger. Makes ¼ cup.

Fall for Fondue

When the weather cools, gather around a bubbling pot (or two) for a convivial, warming way to entertain and eat.

Fireside Beer-Cheese Fondue

Use a beer you'd like to drink in this fondue that takes to a variety of dippers, both sweet and savory.

PREP 25 minutes STAND 30 minutes

WHAT YOU NEED
8   ounces aged white cheddar, Gouda, or Colby cheese, shredded (2 cups)
8   ounces Swiss, Jarlsberg, or Gruyére cheese, shredded (2 cups)
1   shallot, halved, or 1 small onion wedge
2   cloves garlic, halved
1   12-ounce bottle beer or nonalcoholic beer
2   tablespoons cornstarch
2   tablespoons water
½   teaspoon freshly ground white or black pepper
Dippers (such as cooked ham cubes, 1½-inch cubes crusty French or Italian bread, 1½-inch cubes rye or sourdough bread, soft breadsticks torn into chunks, cornichons, jarred cocktail onions, seedless grapes, apple chunks, pear wedges, steamed broccoli or cauliflower florets, and/or cut-up fresh vegetables)

WHAT YOU DO
1. Let shredded cheeses stand at room temperature for 30 minutes. Rub bottom and sides of a heavy 1½- to 3-quart fondue pot with the cut surface of shallot and garlic cloves; discard. Set aside.
2. In a large saucepan heat beer over medium heat until small bubbles rise to the surface. Just before beer boils, reduce heat to low and stir in the cheeses, a little at a time, stirring constantly and making sure cheese melts before adding more. In a small bowl stir together cornstarch, the water, and pepper until well combined. Add to cheese mixture. Cook and whisk until mixture is thickened and bubbly. Transfer cheese mixture to prepared fondue pot. Place over fondue burner.
3. To serve, spear dippers with fondue forks; dip into fondue, swirling to coat. (Fondue will thicken as it holds over the burner. If it becomes too thick, add a little warmed water.) Makes 12 appetizer servings (3 cups fondue).

Tomato, Artichoke, and Olive Fondue

PREP 15 minutes COOK 5 minutes

WHAT YOU NEED
3   cloves garlic, minced
1   shallot, finely chopped
1   tablespoon extra virgin olive oil
1   28-ounce can crushed tomatoes with basil
¼   cup Chianti or other dry red wine (optional)
⅓   cup finely chopped canned artichoke hearts
⅓   cup finely chopped green and/or ripe olives or Kalamata or niçoise olives
⅛   teaspoon cayenne pepper
Dash of salt
Dippers (such as cooked sweet or hot Italian link sausage*; fully cooked smoked sausage, cut into ¾-inch pieces; focaccia or Italian bread cubes, toasted; sticks of mozzarella (string cheese), cut into thirds; sweet pepper wedges; zucchini or yellow summer squash, cut into 2-inch sticks; canned artichoke hearts, halved)

WHAT YOU DO
1. In a large saucepan cook garlic and shallot in hot oil until tender. Stir in tomatoes and wine; heat to boiling. Reduce heat and simmer, uncovered, for 5 minutes. Stir in artichoke hearts, olives, cayenne, and salt. Transfer to fondue pot.
2. Keep warm over medium-low heat. Serve with dippers. Makes 4 servings.
*TIP: To cook sausage, cut into 1-inch lengths. Cook in a larger skillet over medium heat for 8 to 10 minutes or until juices run clear. Drain well in a colander.

Mexican Fondue

PREP 20 minutes SLOW COOK 3 hours (low) or 1½ hours (high)

WHAT YOU NEED
1   14.5-ounce can diced tomatoes, undrained
⅔   cup finely chopped onion
½   cup finely chopped roasted red sweet pepper
1   4-ounce can diced green chile peppers, undrained
3   cups cubed Monterey Jack cheese with salsa or jalapeño peppers or regular Monterey Jack cheese (12 ounces)
3   cups cubed American cheese (12 ounces)
Dippers (such as toasted cubed corn bread* or tortilla wedges)
Milk

WHAT YOU DO
1. In a 3½- or 4-quart slow cooker combine tomatoes, onion, roasted sweet pepper, and chile peppers. Add cheeses; toss gently to combine.
2. Cover and cook on low-heat setting for 3 to 4 hours or on high-heat setting for 1½ to 2 hours. Serve immediately or keep warm, covered, on warm-heat or low-heat setting for up to 2 hours.
3. Serve fondue with dippers, swirling pieces as you dip. If the fondue thickens, stir in a little milk. Makes 36 servings.
*TIP: Purchase corn bread or prepare a packaged corn bread mix.

Swiss Cheese Fondue

This version of classic Swiss cheese fondue is mild enough to suit any palate. Try it with crunchy root vegetable chips.

PREP 5 minutes COOK 10 minutes

WHAT YOU NEED
1½ cups dry white wine
¾   pound Swiss cheese, grated (about 3 cups)
¼   pound mild cheese (such as Monterey Jack), grated (about 1 cup)
¼   teaspoon salt
¼   teaspoon white or black pepper
⅛   teaspoon cayenne pepper
ground nutmeg
2   tablespoons cornstarch blended with 2 tablespoons water
Italian bread, cut into cubes
Granny Smith and Gala apples, cut into chunks
1   7.5-ounce bag mixed root vegetable chips (such as Terra Chips)

WHAT YOU DO
1. Bring wine to a simmer in a flameproof fondue pot or nonaluminum saucepan. Add cheese, stirring until melted; mixture will not be smooth.
2. Stir in salt, pepper, cayenne, and nutmeg. Stir cornstarch-water mixture and add to pot. Simmer over medium-low heat until thickened and smooth, about 2 minutes. Serve immediately with bread chunks, apple pieces, and chips; keep fondue warm over a low flame. Makes 8 servings.

SWISS CHEESE FONDUE

TOMATO, ARTICHOKE,
AND OLIVE FONDUE

FIRESIDE BEER-
CHEESE FONDUE

MEXICAN FONDUE

BITTERSWEET
CHOCOLATE-ORANGE
FONDUE

CHOCOLATE-CARAMEL
FONDUE

CHOCOLATE FONDUE

BUTTERSCOTCH
FONDUE

Bittersweet Chocolate-Orange Fondue

START TO FINISH **15 minutes**

WHAT YOU NEED
6   ounces bittersweet chocolate, coarsely chopped
¾   cup half-and-half or light cream
⅓   cup sugar
¼   cup orange liqueur or orange juice
2   tablespoons honey
    Dippers (such as dried fruits; biscotti cookies; clementines, tangerines, or oranges, peeled and sectioned; pear or apple wedges; whole walnuts, almonds, or pecans)

WHAT YOU DO
1. In a heavy small saucepan melt chocolate over medium-low heat. Whisk in half-and-half until smooth; stir in sugar, orange liqueur, and honey. Cook, stirring constantly, for 4 to 5 minutes or until mixture is slightly thick and sugar dissolves. Transfer to a fondue pot. Keep warm over low heat. Serve with desired dippers. Makes 8 servings.

Chocolate-Caramel Fondue

PREP **10 minutes**
SLOW COOK **2 hours (low)**

WHAT YOU NEED
1   14-ounce can (1¼ cups) sweetened condensed milk
1   12- to 12.5-ounce container caramel ice cream topping
9   ounces semisweet chocolate, coarsely chopped, or 1½ cups semisweet chocolate pieces
    Dippers (such as angel food or pound cake cubes, large marshmallows, dried apricots, or fresh fruit including strawberries, banana slices, and/or pineapple chunks)
    Milk (optional)

WHAT YOU DO
1. In a 1½-quart slow cooker stir together sweetened condensed milk, ice cream topping, and chocolate.
2. Cover and cook on low-heat setting for 2 hours. Stir until mixture is smooth. Serve immediately or keep warm, covered, on low-heat setting for up to 1 hour (chocolate mixture will become grainy if held longer).
3. To serve, spear dippers with fondue forks. Dip into chocolate mixture, swirling as you dip. If the mixture thickens, stir in a little warm milk to make fondue desired consistency. Makes 12 servings.

Butterscotch Fondue

A pot of this buttery-tasting fondue is nice to have as an option to chocolate—and it's so simple to put together, you can serve both: Just combine everything in the slow cooker, cover, and heat, stirring occasionally.

PREP **10 minutes**
SLOW COOK **3 hours (low)**

2   14-ounce cans sweetened condensed milk
2   cups packed brown sugar
1   cup butter, melted
⅔   cup light corn syrup
1   teaspoon vanilla
¼   cup rum or milk
    Apple slices, whole strawberries, cubed sponge cake, cookies, and/or cubed brownies

WHAT YOU DO
1. In a 3½- or 4-quart slow cooker stir together the sweetened condensed milk, brown sugar, melted butter, corn syrup, and vanilla.
2. Cover and cook on low-heat setting for 3 hours (do not cook on high-heat setting). Whisk in rum until smooth. Keep warm on low-heat setting for up to 2 hours, stirring occasionally.
3. Serve with apple slices, strawberries, sponge cake, cookies, and/or brownies. Makes 21 (¼-cup) servings.

Chocolate Fondue

Check out the liqueur-infused, peanut butter, mocha, and white chocolate variations on this ever-popular dessert below.

START TO FINISH **15 minutes**

WHAT YOU NEED
8   ounces semisweet chocolate, coarsely chopped
1   14-ounce can (1¼ cups) sweetened condensed milk
⅓   cup milk
    Dippers (such as angel food or pound cake cubes, brownie squares, marshmallows, whole strawberries, banana slices, pineapple chunks, or dried apricots)

WHAT YOU DO
1. In a medium heavy saucepan heat and stir chocolate over low heat until melted. Stir in sweetened condensed milk and milk; heat through. Transfer to a fondue pot; keep warm.
2. Serve fondue sauce immediately with assorted dippers. Swirl pieces as you dip. If the fondue mixture thickens, stir in some additional milk.
Chocolate-Liqueur Fondue: Prepare as above, except stir 2 to 4 tablespoons amaretto, orange, hazelnut, or cherry liqueur into mixture after heating.
Chocolate-Peanut Fondue: Prepare as above, except stir ½ cup creamy peanut butter in with the milk.
Mocha Fondue: Prepare as above, except substitute ⅓ cup strong brewed coffee for the milk.
White Chocolate Fondue: Prepare as above, except substitute white chocolate baking squares for semisweet chocolate and add one 7-ounce jar marshmallow creme to the saucepan with the chocolate. Reduce milk to 2 tablespoons. After fondue is smooth and melted, stir in ¼ cup creme de cacao or amaretto.

An evening featuring cheese and chocolate is sure to be a success, especially when the cooking and serving method is stir, dip, swirl, and eat!

Easy Does It
Frozen Treats

Sherbet Fruit Pops

Arrange 10 5-ounce paper cups on a baking pan. In a small bowl combine 3 peeled and chopped kiwifruit and 1 tablespoon sugar. Divide chopped kiwifruits among cups. In a large bowl using an electric mixer on low speed beat together 1 quart of raspberry or tangerine sherbet and 2 to 4 tablespoons orange juice until combined. Spoon sherbet mixture over kiwi, filling in cups. Cover cups with foil. Cut a slit in each foil top. Insert wooden crafts sticks. Freeze at least 6 hours or overnight. Makes 10 pops. *TIP: Use almost any fruit you like, such as chopped peaches, berries, or grapes.

Fruity White Sangria Pops

In a small saucepan combine ⅓ cup sugar and ⅓ cup water. Bring to boiling, stirring to dissolve sugar. Add 1 cup dry white wine. Return to boiling. Reduce heat. Add 1 cup sliced fresh strawberries and ¾ cup chopped mango. Simmer 2 minutes. Remove from heat. Drain, reserving fruit and cooking liquid. Cool slightly. In a small bowl combine drained fruit, 2 peeled and thinly sliced kiwifruits, and ½ cup green halved or quartered green grapes. Divide fruit among 12 frozen pop molds or 12 3-ounce paper cups. In a small pitcher combine 1 cup reserved cooking liquid, ¼ cup ginger ale, and 1 tablespoon lime juice. Pour ginger ale mixture over fruit in cups. Add pop mold sticks (or cover cups with foil and add wooden crafts sticks). Freeze for 6 to 24 hours or until firm. Makes 12 pops.

Frozen Yogurt Pops

In a large bowl combine 2 cups low-fat vanilla yogurt; 1 12-ounce can juice concentrate, such as grape, raspberry, fruit blend, orange, or lemonade; and ½ teaspoon vanilla.** Divide mixture among 8 (5-ounce) paper cups. Cover cups with foil. Cut a slit in each foil top. Insert wooden crafts sticks. Freeze overnight or until firm. Makes 8 pops. **TIP: For a swirled effect, make two different batches using two different 6-ounce juice concentrates. Pour a little of each in each cup, stirring just briefly before freezing.

Melon-Berry Smoothie Pops

In a blender combine 1 cup frozen unsweetened whole strawberries, 1 cup cut-up cantaloupe, ⅓ cup orange juice, ¼ cup fat-free milk, and 1 tablespoon honey. Cover and blend until smooth. Stir in 1 cup calorie-free citrus-flavor sparkling water. Pour mixture into 12 3-ounce frozen pop molds and cover. (Or pour into 12 3-ounce plastic cups. Cover cups with foil. Cut a slit in each top. Insert wooden crafts sticks.) Freeze for about 4 hours or until firm. Makes 12 pops.

Layered Frozen Chocolate-Coffee Pops

Stir together 1 4-serving-siz package white chocolate instant pudding mix and 1¼ teaspoons instant espresso powder. Add 2 cups fat-free milk. Whisk until smooth and thick. Spoon into 8 5-ounce paper cups; chill. Whisk together ⅓ cup sweetened condensed milk; ¼ cup unsweetened cocoa powder; ½ teaspoon instant espresso powder; and ½ teaspoon vanilla. Whisk in 1½ cups water. Spoon over pudding layer in cups. Cover with foil and insert wooden crafts sticks as above. Freeze at least 12 hours or until firm. Makes 8 pops.

summer

A WALK IN THE PARK

ENJOY IT

Warm and wonderful—summer is filled with reasons to celebrate. Make the most of the sunshine season with these clever ideas leading the way.

Dear Ol' Dad

Show your love for Dad with thoughtful gifts and
wraps that will long be remembered.

Surprise Package

Dad will love this clever gift wrap you
make yourself. Create a custom stamp
by wrapping twine around a plain acrylic
or wooden block, securing the twine
ends to the back of the block using tape.
Press the stamp onto the ink pad; then
experiment with different color and size
combinations to stamp on crafts or solid-
color wrapping papers.

Pattern Play

Stencil a handsome set of coasters that will make Dad's at-home game watching just that more enjoyable. Cut 4-inch squares from thin cork. Cut a simple herringbone pattern from stencil acetate. Press the stencil onto a cork square and apply acrylic paint in his favorite colors; let dry.

Game On

Buy Dad tickets to see his favorite team. Nestle the tickets in a shallow container filled with peanuts and tie with string. If wrapping the gift, slip it into a cellophane sleeve and tie the ends closed.

String It On

It's colorful, fresh, and versatile. Use baker's twine to give projects the sweet treatment.

Too Cute to Eat

Mix up a batch of decorative mini cupcakes by winding twine around small foam balls. Use a quick-drying glue, such as Fabri-Tac, to keep the twine in place. Then top with pretty pins, beads, brads, or paper punches and place in paper baking cups.

Bright Bouquet

Plant a garden of colorful blooms by embellishing punched flower shapes with baker's twine. To make the base for each flower, use a punch to make shape from colored cardstock as shown in Photo A. Tape end of baker's twine to one side of scallop circle as shown in Photo B. Wrap twine around circle, fitting it in scallops as you work around circle and crossing through center with each wrap as shown in Photo C. Trim the end of the twine and tape it in place on the back of the circle. Thread twine into a large-eye sewing needle and stitch through the holes in the center of a button. If desired, use a small scallop circle punch to make a smaller flower and hot-glue it to the center of a large one. Hot-glue the button to the center of the flower and one end of the wire to the back of the flower for a stem.

Novel Idea

Accent a purchased fabric-covered stretch headband with a felt flower topped with a baker's twine pom-pom for a colorful bookmark. Use the pattern on page 157 to cut three petal shapes from felt for the flower. To make a pom-pom, wrap baker's twine around the tines of a fork approximately 35 times, securing the beginning of the twine under the wraps. Cut the twine from the spool as shown in Photo A. Cut a 12-inch length of twine. Insert it between the center tines, and tie it into a single knot around the middle of the wrapped twine as shown in Photo B. Pull the wrapped twine off the tines of the fork. Tighten the knot around the center of the wraps and tie it again to make a double knot as shown in Photo C. Insert scissors through each loop on both sides of the tie, and cut through the loops. Arrange the felt petals into a circle and use the twin tails to stitch through the center and onto the headband.

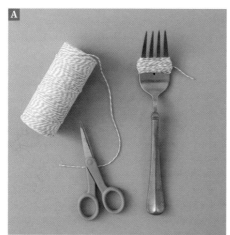
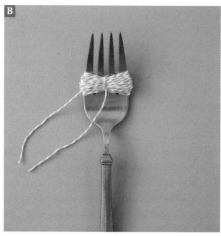
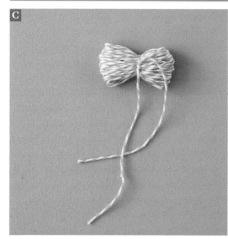
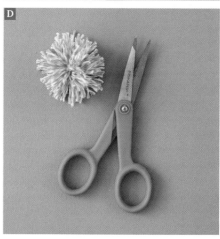

Up, Up, and Away

Let your creativity take flight on a greeting card. Use the pattern on page 157 to cut the balloon shapes from scrapbook papers; glue twine to the front of the balloon to make the segments. Connect the balloon basket with short twine lengths, tucking the ends behind the shapes. Glue to the front of a blank 5×7-inch card and add a sticker message.

Power of Red

Make a tiered centerpiece that bursts with red flowers. Center florist's foam in three white enamel containers or other graduated-size vessels. Pour water over the foam, allowing some standing water. Stack containers and press blooms, such as the dahlias shown, into the florist's foam to cover.

Playfully Patriotic

Let freedom ring with vintage-inspired projects.

Just Coasting

Message coasters protect the table and extend warm wishes all at once. For easy assembly, start with blank 4-inch-diameter chipboard coasters. Print out coaster-size circular 4th of July clip art onto white cardstock and cut out. Spray chipboard coasters with spray adhesive and press cut-out designs to adhere. Spray with clear finish and let dry.

Bundle of Fun

Independence Day guests will love collecting their sparkler wands, especially when wrapped in festive sleeves. Using the photo for inspiration, cut star and banner shapes out of red, white, and blue cardstock. Use a crafts knife to cut slits along the white dotted lines. Slide four sparklers through the slits so the words show on top of the sparklers. Be sure to remove the sparklers from the paper holders before lighting.

True Colors

Honor the grand old flag with party decor that's all about stripes. Spider mums and ruffly carnations burst from a vase like fireworks. Ribbon-wrapped matchboxes and votive candleholders are easy-to-make take-home gifts for guests.

Birthday Treats

Offer cupfuls of sweets packaged in floral boxes in shades of red and blue. Cut two 3×9-inch strips of double-sided scrapbook paper and overlap in a cross shape; use a glue stick to adhere overlapped centers. Punch a hole in the corners of each strip. Fold sides up and thread ribbon or rickrack through the holes to shape the box together. Fill with lightweight snacks that won't slip through the open edges. For smaller treats, line the box with a cellophane food bag.

Roll Call

This multitasking place mat with flatware holder is made from a dish towel. It rolls up for grab-and-go ease, then unfurls to stand in for a tablecloth. Fold the long edge of a dishtowel to about the size of a place mat. Stitch or hot-glue to create a utensil pocket on the left side. Insert utensils in the pocket, roll up, and tie a ribbon around to secure.

Pinwheel Parade

Wave a parade of whirling pinwheels to hand out as party favors. Cut scrapbook paper into 12- and 6-inch squares. Fold paper square in half diagonally, fold in half again to form a triangle, then unfold. Cut each creased line to within ¼ inch of center. Fold every other point to the center, slightly overlapping tips and securing with tape. For center, cut a round piece from complementary paper and press a map tack through it. Insert the tack through the pinwheel center and thread a bead onto the tack. (The bead acts as a spacer between the pinwheel and dowel to allow spinning.) Press tack into a dowel that has had one end soaked in water to make it pliable. Display in sand-filled containers.

Made in the U.S.A.

Salute Old Glory with star-studded napkin rings. Use a steel stamp set to hammer U.S.A. into metal tags. Insert ribbons through tags and wrap around striped napkins.

Whimsy in the Garden

Let flea market finds blossom into clever, one-of-a-kind garden creations. There's no telling what you might come up with when you open up your imagination.

Flower Burst Trellis

Plant some oversize blooms that catch the sunlight like glass. Once kitchen serving pieces, these plastic shapes combine to resemble a joyous bouquet to be enjoyed from afar. Look for pieces such as scallop-edge bowls, chip dishes, hard-boiled egg platters, coasters, strainers, glass lids, and glasses. Translucent pieces give the look of colored glass. If you find clear pieces, dust the back with a light coat of spray paint and let dry. Layer the pieces to add dimension to flower centers and glue in place with a sturdy glue suitable for the outdoors. Let the glue dry. Arrange the blooms on a trellis and glue in place.

Posy Party

What a lovely vintage addition to landscaping. Candleholders, bowls, coffee filters, and more make up this flowery bunch. Use an all-weather adhesive to attach pieces together, adding butter knife stems if needed.

Friendly Fellow

Well-used kitchen gadgets and baking pans give this guy
personality plus. Use the photograph for inspiration, then scour
secondhand shops for odds and ends of metal pieces that could
combine to make your own backyard friend. Use screws to hold
the pieces together, drilling holes when needed. Be sure to wear
safety goggles when drilling and gloves to handle any sharp
items.

Shirley

Here's a sweetie that's sure to bring giggles in the garden. With a flip-flopped coffeepot head and two-bowl body, this gal is full of surprises. Her details are what give her style, such as cookie press eyes, tart pan buttons, and photo holder hair. To connect the components, drill holes and wire pieces together. For a more temporary hold, use thick double-sided tape to keeps shape intact.

Fred

With a built-in smile, this happy
gentleman is a cinch to put
together. His body is an old
gas can; his head is made from
a paint can with the handle
forming his smile. Roller-skate-
wheel eyes and a cookie cutter
nose add to his character. Tuck
metal shoe forms underneath for
feet and a layered tin hat and this
guy's ready to hit the town.

Junior

Hey, little fella! So simple and so darn cute, this garden charmer is made of just four pieces—a toy phone for the head, a play dustpan for the body, and a pair of partial roller skates for the legs. If you find a phone without bells, try using wheels, bottle caps, or cookie cutters for eyes.

No Watering Needed

Woven baskets, plate chargers, and more give these flower heads lots of fun texture. Glue the pieces together using a strong adhesive suitable for outdoors. Leaf-shape serving pieces and walking canes complete the larger-than-life blooms.

What's the Buzz

You won't want to run from this bee he's just too adorable! With a pair of tennis racket wings attached to a wall sconce body and a strainer head with roller skate eyes and knob nose, he'll get nothing but favorable attention hanging about your yard.

New-Bee

A smaller version, this flying friend is composed from kitchen drawer finds. The bumper eyes are attached with screws, hiding the nuts on the back side. His mismatched wings are part of his everlasting charm.

Easy Does It
Simply Paint

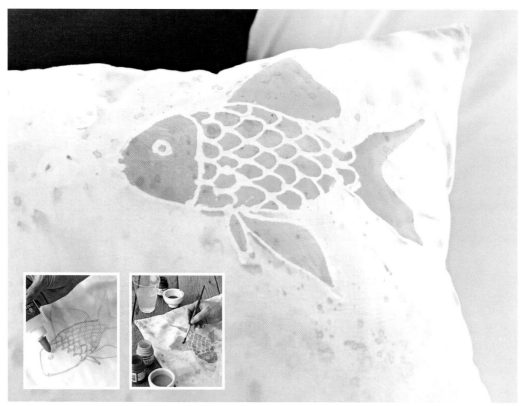

Gone Fishing

Float a bright fish on a pillow sham to embellish an aquatic bedroom theme. Make a fish pattern from clip art or a freehand sketch. Outline with a bold black marking pen. Place the pattern inside the sham and trace it with washable white glue to create a mask. When dry, brush on color using slightly watered-down fabric paint. Once dry, soak sham in water and gently rub away glue. To set design, follow the fabric paint directions.

Watered Down

Turn a plain duvet into a piece of art. Wet the duvet with water, then spread it out on a flat surface. Mix water and fabric paint until watery. Drench a large paintbrush with the mixture and fling it at the duvet, allowing the paint to run and bleed. The colors will lightly bleed through to the back layer of fabric. When dry, use a bottle fitted with a tip that has a small opening and filled with the water-paint mixture to paint circles, lines, and dots.

Light Waves

Add a splash of personality to a boring lampshade. Moisten a large paintbrush with water and sweep a wavelike pattern around bottom of shade. Tap wet paint into the pattern with a soft round watercolor brush, using watercolor paint for paper lampshades and fabric paint for fabric shades. The paint will bleed to the edges of the moistened area. After the paint dries, dot the wave with more paint to create stronger tones amid the soft background.

Stripes Ahoy

Transport dinner guests to a coastal retreat with a table setting anchored by nautically inspired napkins. Combine fabric paint and water until the mixture achieves a watery consistency. Paint stripes across napkins using a flat brush. The color should bleed slightly to achieve the tie-dyed appearance.

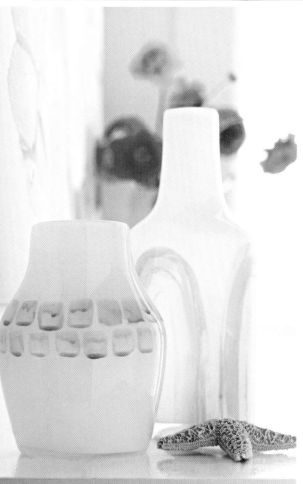

Glass Act

Bring the seaside tableside by adding cool color to salvaged vases. Peruse thrift shop shelves for milky white vases in various shapes and sizes. To achieve a watercolor effect on glass, mix glass paint with a few drops of paint thinner. If desired, adjust the amount of paint thinner to achieve varying viscosities and results, such as drips and runs. Paint freehand designs on each vase and let dry.

boo!

HAUNT AWAY

Celebrate this Halloween with a cauldron full of party and decorating ideas that make trick-or-treating worth repeating.

Black and White Magic

With a classic palette and clever touches, this Halloween party is surprisingly sophisticated yet suitably unsettling.

Elevated Taste

You will not be making pumpkin pie with this latex version, but you will get the compliments. Embellish with a laser-cut sticker and strips of adhesive black jewels and display on a black candleholder.

Tier-ful Repast
Layers of detail make this spirited table a visual feast. A garland of black leaves skirts the table, a spiderweb covers the surface, and place settings are anchored with blackboard oilcloth mats.

Sinister Sideboard

A study in black and white graces the top of a white beaded sideboard. Fill apothecary jars with black jelly beans and black-and-white candy sticks. Wrap newspaper or yellowed pages from an old book with twine to create a hangout for plastic spiders. Spanish moss topping a vintage urn (or simply spread across the table) provides an overgrown look.

Tricky Treats

Like positive and negative space, these treat bags mirror each other and hold the promise of tasty morsels. To satisfy everyone's sweet tooth, pack the bags with a nutty caramel corn mixture, gather them on a tray, and place a large apothecary jar nearby filled with white chocolate- or yogurt-covered candies.

Helping Hand

Set each plate with a handmade place card presented in, appropriately enough, a hand. Lay the place settings on mats fashioned from blackboard oilcloth. To make the mats, cut a 1×12-inch rectangle from oilcloth using pinking shears or decorative-edge scissors.

Well Urned

A stately raven stands sentinel over a jet-black urn decorating the center of the table. Use black matte spray paint to get the same look for a purchased plastic or metal urn. Fill the urn with Spanish moss and top with "soil" made from chocolate wafers ground in a food processor.

Get Your Ghoul On

Welcome guests to sit a spell
while quirky characters
meander about.

Enter If You Dare

What a fun way to invite guests over for Halloween tricks and treats. Paint an unfinished frame black and brush with a light coat of silver. Write party information on white cardstock cut to fit frame. Chalk the edges with black and hot-glue to back side of frame. Trim a corner with a multiribbon bow. Add a wire for hanging—long for a doorknob or short for a nail. Make an additional invitation to display the night of the party so guests know they have arrived at the right mansion.

Among Friends

Set the table for four and invite a slew more! This Halloween table setting has so many interesting details, guests will want to linger long after the last pumpkin bar is stolen away.

Plate People

To make a ghoulish face plate, cut two 2-inch, one 3-inch, and one 8-inch circle from white cardstock. Using black chalk and an applicator, darken the edges of each circle as shown in Photo A. Use the patterns, page 158 to cut the mouth and nostrils from black paper. Cut a ½- and a 1-inch circle from black. Using the photos as guides, adhere the pieces in place using a glue stick. Top each with a clear glass plate before dining. Replace the string in an eye mask with ¾-inch-wide black and white ribbon. Just overlap the mask onto the character and tuck the ribbons under the clear glass plate.

Halloween Frame-Up

Open-center place mats add to the wonderful peculiarity of this tabletop. Start with a flat scroll-edge picture frame from the crafts store. Using black acrylic paint, coat the top and edges; let dry. With very little silver paint on a fan-shape paintbrush, "dust" the frame surface in X strokes. Let the paint dry.

Neat Trick Is a Treat

A Halloween brad creates a pocket for silverware in a jiffy. Poke it through a plastic flower trim before securing it through the napkin layers. Jagged spaghetti forks are in keeping with the spooky atmosphere of the party.

Place Marker Candy Cup

An initial sticker on a metal-framed paper tag identifies guests' places at the table. Thread onto a length of black craft wire and spiral around a dowel or skewer. Make a loop at the end and tape it to the center of a cupcake liner. Fill with treats for a place marker.

Kinda Cute, Kinda Creepy

This clan has Halloween written all over it.

WHAT YOU'LL NEED

clean, hard, dry bottle or can, such as from
  hairspray
plastic foam ball to fit bottle as desired plus 1- to
  ½-inch balls for stacked trio
adhesive for plastic foam
6-inch-long wood skewer
papier mâché mix
water
large mixing bowl
paint stir stick
black wire
wire cutter
small plier
face pieces, such as map pins, upholstery tacks,
  O-rings, and rubber washers
quick-set adhesive, such as CA
acrylic paint in black, copper, and white
paintbrushes in ¾-inch flat and small round
  detail brush
pushpin

WHAT YOU DO

1. Press the plastic foam ball onto the top of the
bottle to impress the opening into the ball;
remove as shown in Photo A. Glue ball onto
bottle and let dry.
2. Following the manufacturer's directions, mix
the papier mâché powder with water in a bowl.
Stir with paint stick until an oatmeal-like
consistency as shown in Photo B. Use hands to
smear entire form with papier mâché as shown in
Photo C. Smooth paste as much as possible; let
dry thoroughly.
3. Decide how to arrange shapes on face. Photo D
shows some examples of items to use.
4. Press pins and tacks into face where desired.
Glue rings and washers onto ghoul's face; let dry.
5. Paint the entire ghoul and features with black
paint as shown in Photo E; let dry.
6. Paint the body portion with white or copper,
allowing some of the black crevices to show
through as shown in Photo F. Avoid painting the
eye and nose areas. Use a detail brush to paint
white onto face area around facial details as
shown in Photo G. Let the paint dry.
7. For mouth, shape pieces of wire into the
desired shape, such as a long curve for the smile
with intersecting staple shapes. Leave ¼-inch
tails to poke into head. For starter holes for long
wire, poke into foam using a pushpin as shown in
Photo H. Insert long wire; if it feels loose,
remove and put a drop of glue in each hole and
reinsert. Repeat for short intersecting wires as
shown in Photos I and J.
8. For stacked trio on stick, thread plastic foam
balls onto a skewer and repeat Steps 2 through 7.

Mr. Expressionist

Welcome partygoers with a goofy pumpkin hanging for all to see. If Halloween crafting is a family affair, offer a variety of wood pieces and see who comes up with the most interesting face.

WHAT YOU'LL NEED

smooth wood plate
wood J for stem
drill and small bit
wire
wood pieces, such as Os, wheels, checkers, golf tees, teardrops, small craft sticks, triangles, and beads
quick-dry glue, such as CA
acrylic paint in black, copper, and white
paintbrush

WHAT YOU DO

1. Drill a hole through the top of the plate, 1 inch from the edge as shown in Photo A.
2. Thread hole with wire and secure to make a hanging loop by twisting the ends together as shown in Photo B.
3. Decide placement of pieces as shown in Photos C through F. Glue stem over wire to hide it.
4. Glue pieces together as shown in Photo G. Glue to pumpkin. Let glue dry.
5. Paint around each detail with black as shown in Photo H; let dry.
6. Paint the main areas copper, allowing a narrow edge of black to show. Paint loosely, without making edges straight as shown in Photo I; let dry.
7. Using the photo for inspiration, highlight details with white paint as shown in Photo J. Let the paint dry.
8. If desired, hang a "place mat" frame (see page 123) behind the pumpkin.

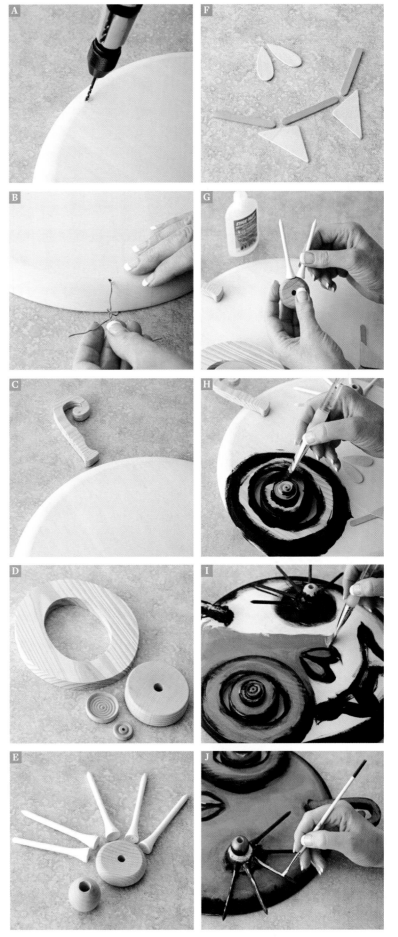

Posh Pumpkins

Skip the scare. These genius ideas turn no-carve pumpkins
into stylish Halloween decor.

Fanciful Duo

Fluttering butterflies alight on
pumpkins in the attractive fall
centerpiece. Spray-paint faux
butterflies from a crafts store
black for a sophisticated look, then
trim their wires to press into the
pumpkin's skin. A harlequinlike mask
adds whimsy.

Jester Time

Mini pumpkins get a timely topping with paper stars in Halloween tones slipped over the stems. Computer-generate an 8-pointed star or use clip art in a size that's approximately ½ inch bigger around than the pumpkin width. Punch a hole in the center and slip it over the stem; cut larger if necessary. Add a smaller layer, if desired,– using a floral or round punch to make the shape. To secure the points, press upholstery tacks into each tip.

Fresh Flowers

Looking for a design you can use all autumn long? Put a fresh spin on your pumpkins with daisy designs. Use an apple corer to cut flower centers and a triangle clay loop tool to carve petal designs.

Knock-Out Punch

A plunger-type apple corer lets you tap out circles from an assortment of pumpkins and winter squashes. Mix and match the multicolored circles to create polka-dot patterns.

Stack of Three

Choose three flat-bottom pumpkins in graduated sizes and different colors (no need to hollow them out). Using a ¾-inch hole-saw bit, drill circles in desired pattern. Switch drilled plugs between pumpkins of different colors. If desired, push the plugs slightly below the skin for a 3-D effect. Use a woodcarving gouge or tip of a vegetable peeler to cut random swirls.

Berriboned Beauties

Trendy animal-print ribbon and duct tape dress pumpkins in fashion-forward style. The white gourd features stripes of black electrical tape and zebra duct tape. Tiger- and leopard-print ribbon segments fit between grooves to form a checkerboard (applied with fabric glue) on the large orange pumpkin.

All Hallows' Eats

Start fright night out right with this pre-trick-or-treating spread of spooky nibbles and scary sips that will fill them up before they head out.

MEATY MUMMIES,
page 136

Tombstone Taco Dip

PREP 15 minutes CHILL 30 minutes
BAKE 5 minutes OVEN 350°F

WHAT YOU NEED

1   16-ounce can refried beans with green
    chiles
¼   cup bottled salsa
⅔   cup bottled ranch salad dressing
2   teaspoons taco seasoning
1½ cups finely chopped cooked chicken
1   7-ounce pouch refrigerated guacamole
½   of a 2.25-ounce can chopped pitted ripe
    olives, drained
    Tortilla Graveyard Characters (see below)
    Shredded lettuce
    Tortilla chips
    10-inch flour tortillas (any flavor)

WHAT YOU DO

1. In a small bowl combine refried beans and salsa.
Spread refried bean mixture in a 2-quart
rectangular dish. In a small bowl combine ranch
salad dressing and taco seasoning; stir in chicken.
2. Spoon on top of the beans in an even layer.
Spoon guacamole in small mounds on top of the
chicken mixture. Carefully spread to an even layer.
3. Cover and chill at least 30 minutes or up to
6 hours before serving. Just before serving, place
Graveyard Characters into dip. Sprinkle the graves
with chopped olives and shredded lettuce.
4. Serve with tortilla chips.

Tortilla Graveyard Characters: Using cookie
cutters or a knife, cut tortillas into gravestones,
cats, owls, bats, fence rails, and a tree. Bake in a
350°F oven for 5 to 7 minutes or until firm and
crisp. Cool on rack.

WICKED WITCH HATS

APPLE CIDER PUNCH

Meaty Mummies

START TO FINISH 45 minutes

WHAT YOU NEED

12 small purchased meatballs, cooked and cooled
12 4-inch lengths of thin summer sausage
12 6-inch wooden skewers
8   ounces cream cheese, softened
1   teaspoon purchased pesto
6   ounces dry fettuccine
    Capers
2   cups marinara sauce, warmed

WHAT YOU DO

1. Place a meatball and a piece of summer sausage on each wooden skewer.
2. In a small bowl combine cream cheese and pesto; set aside. Cook fettuccine according to package directions. Drain and let sit until cool enough to handle.
3. Spread a little cream cheese on each meat skewer and wrap with cooked fettuccine noodles. Spread a little more cream cheese mixture on the skewer and wrap with another layer of fettuccine. Add 2 capers to each skewer for eyes.
4. Serve with pasta sauce for dipping.

Wicked Witch Hats

PREP 30 minutes STAND 30 minutes
CHILL 4 hours

WHAT YOU NEED

1   8-ounce package cream cheese
1   cup finely shredded Mexican-blend cheese (4 ounces)

¼   cup butter
1   tablespoon milk
½   teaspoon Worcestershire sauce
2   tablespoons thinly sliced green onion
2   tablespoons chopped bottled green jalapeños or diced green chiles, drained
¾   cup finely crushed round blue corn tortilla chips (2½ cups)
20 round blue corn tortilla chips
2   to 3 long carrots, peeled

WHAT YOU DO

1. In a large bowl let cream cheese, shredded cheese, and butter stand at room temperature for 30 minutes. Add milk and Worcestershire sauce. Beat with an electric mixer on medium until fluffy. Stir in green onion and jalapeños. Cover and chill for 4 to 24 hours.
2. Shape chilled cheese mixture into 1-inch balls, using about 1 tablespoon mixture for each; mold balls into cone shapes. Roll cones in crushed blue corn chips, pressing lightly to adhere.
3. Using a vegetable peeler, cut carrots into thin strips. Cut strips into narrow pieces. Wrap a carrot strip around each cone to form a hatband.* Place each cone on a tortilla chip to create hat brims; serve immediately. Or cover and refrigerate up to 1 hour; place on hat brims just before serving. Makes 20 hats.
Make-Ahead Tip: Prepare as directed in Step 1. Wrap cheese ball in plastic wrap. Freeze up to 1 month. When ready to assemble, thaw cheese ball in the

refrigerator overnight. Let stand for 15 minutes at room temperature. Unwrap and shape as directed.
*Tie the carrot strip in a loose knot or use cheese-ball mixture to secure the hatband.

Apple Cider Punch

This bubbly cider punch is adaptable to be all-ages friendly or for adults only. Make it with sparkling white grape juice, sparkling wine, or champagne.

START TO FINISH 5 minutes

WHAT YOU NEED

6   cups apple cider
2   cups orange juice, cranberry-raspberry juice, or orange-mango juice
½   cup lemon juice
1   750-milliliter bottle sparkling white grape juice, sparkling wine, or champagne
    Orange and/or black licorice sticks (optional)

WHAT YOU DO

1. In punch bowl, large pitcher, or pitchers combine apple cider, orange juice, and lemon juice. Slowly add sparkling white grape juice, wine, or champagne. Garnish each glass with a licorice stick if desired. Serve immediately. Makes about 15 (6-ounce) servings.

Worm-Crusted Eyeball Pie

Eeww! Your dinner looks back at you! (And it tastes good too!)

PREP 10 minutes COOK 10 minutes
BAKE 30 minutes STAND 5 minutes
OVEN 350°F

WHAT YOU NEED

- 4 ounces dried spaghetti
- 1 tablespoon butter
- 1 egg, beaten
- ¼ cup grated Parmesan cheese
- 8 ounces lean ground beef or bulk Italian sausage
- ½ cup chopped onion (1 medium)
- ½ cup chopped green sweet pepper (½ of a pepper)
- 1 clove garlic, minced
- 1 8-ounce can tomato sauce
- 1 teaspoon dried oregano, crushed Nonstick cooking spray
- 1 cup low-fat cottage cheese, drained
- 1 8-ounce container 1-inch fresh mozzarella balls, drained
- 12 to 16 medium ripe olives, drained and halved

WHAT YOU DO

1. Cook spaghetti according to package directions; drain.
2. Return spaghetti to warm saucepan. Stir butter into hot pasta until melted. Stir in egg and Parmesan cheese; set aside.
3. Meanwhile, in a medium skillet cook ground beef or Italian sausage, onion, sweet pepper, and garlic until meat is brown and onion is tender. Drain. Stir in tomato sauce and oregano; heat through.
4. Coat a 9-inch pie plate with nonstick cooking spray. Press spaghetti mixture onto bottom and up sides of pie plate, forming a crust. Spread cottage cheese on the top and up the sides of pasta crust. Spread meat mixture over cottage cheese.
5. Bake, uncovered, in a 350°F oven for 25 minutes or until heated through. Remove from oven; arrange the mozzarella balls over top of pie. Return to oven; bake 5 minutes or until cheese is softened. Remove from oven and add an olive half to each mozzarella ball to complete eyeballs. Let stand 5 minutes. To serve, cut into wedges. Makes 6 servings.

No Tricks, Just Treats

These not-so-scary homemade Halloween sweets beat bagged candy, hands down.

GHOSTLY CUPCAKES,
page 140

CREAMY HALLOWEENY
PUSH-UP POPS, page 140

Ghostly Cupcakes

START TO FINISH 45 minutes

WHAT YOU NEED

12 2½-inch White Chocolate Cupcakes or other 2½-inch white cupcakes in paper bake cups
1 16-ounce can vanilla frosting
12 1¾-inch White Chocolate Cupcakes or other white cupcakes
12 small glazed or plain doughnut holes
16 ounces purchased white rolled fondant
Black candy-coated sunflower kernels or 1 tube black icing

WHAT YOU DO

1. Set the 2½-inch White Chocolate Cupcakes on a flat surface; generously pipe some of the frosting on each cupcake. If necessary, remove paper bake cups from the 1¾-inch White Chocolate Cupcakes. Place, upside down, on tops of the large cupcakes. Generously pipe some frosting on top of each small cupcake. Top each with a doughnut hole. If desired, pipe a little frosting on the tops of the doughnut holes. If necessary, use frosting to secure any unstable parts of stacks.
2. Shape purchased fondant into 1½-inch-diameter balls. (Work with one ball of fondant at a time and keep remaining fondant covered until needed.) On parchment paper, roll one ball into a 6-inch-diameter circle. Drape fondant circle loosely over a cupcake stack, pressing or creasing the fondant in places to make the stack look more ghostly. Repeat to make 12 ghostly cupcakes.
3. For faces, use frosting to attach sunflower kernels to fondant for eyes and mouths or use black icing to pipe eyes and mouths. Makes 12 (2½-inch) cupcakes.

White Chocolate Cupcakes: Preheat oven to 350°F. Line sixteen 2-½-inch and twelve 1¾-inch muffin cups with white paper bake cups. In a large mixing bowl beat 4 ounces softened cream cheese with an electric mixer until fluffy. Add one package 2-layer-size white cake mix, 1 cup milk, ½ cup vegetable oil, and 4 eggs. Beat on medium speed for 2 minutes, scraping sides of bowl occasionally. Stir in 1 cup finely chopped white baking chocolate or miniature white baking pieces. Spoon batter into muffin cups, filling each about three-fourths full. Bake about 20 minutes for 2½-inch cupcakes, about 14 minutes for 1¾-inch cupcakes, or until a wooden toothpick inserted in centers comes out clean. Cool cupcakes in muffin cups on wire racks for 10 minutes. Remove cupcakes from muffin cups. Cool completely on wire racks.

Creamy Halloweeny Push-Up Pops

PREP 45 minutes   BAKE 18 minutes
COOL 15 minutes   OVEN 350°F

WHAT YOU NEED

1 package 2-layer-size white cake mix
½ teaspoon ground ginger
2 teaspoons yellow liquid food coloring
1 4-serving-size package vanilla instant pudding and pie filling mix
1¼ cups milk
1 tablespoon orange juice concentrate, thawed
Orange paste food coloring
4 ounces cream cheese, softened
3 cups powdered sugar
15 push-up containers

WHAT YOU DO

1. Preheat oven to 350°F. Grease two 8×8×2-inch baking pans. Line pan bottoms with parchment paper or waxed paper. Grease paper; set pans aside. Prepare cake mix according to package directions, adding the ground ginger before beating. Divide batter in half. Tint half the batter with yellow food coloring. Spread yellow batter into one pan. Spread plain batter into remaining pan. Bake for 18 to 20 minutes or until cakes springs back when lightly touched. Cool in pans on a wire rack for 15 minutes. Remove cakes from pans; cool completely on wire racks. Transfer to a cutting board.*
2. For orange filling, prepare pudding according to package directions except use 1¼ cups of milk for liquid. Stir in orange juice concentrate. Tint with orange food coloring. Cover and chill until ready to assemble.
3. For cream cheese filling, in a medium mixing bowl beat the cream cheese with an electric mixer on medium to high speed for 30 seconds. Gradually beat in powdered sugar until well combined. Spoon cream cheese filling into a pastry bag fitted with a large round or star tip; spoon orange pudding filling into another pastry bag fitted with a large round tip.
4. Using the open end of a push-up container as a cutter, cut out 15 circles from each cake (cut the circles as close together as possible). Pipe 1 teaspoon of cream cheese filling in the bottom of each push-up container. Place one yellow cake circle in each container. Pipe orange filling on top. Add a white cake circle and top with 1 tablespoon of cream cheese filling. Place the top on each container. Store in the refrigerator for up to 2 days. Makes 15 cake pops.
*For easier cutting, freeze the cake layers for 20 to 30 minutes.

No-Bake Spiderweb Cheesecakes

These pretty little individual cheesecakes go together in a flash and can be made the day before you need them.

PREP 10 minutes   MICROWAVE 30 seconds plus 1 minute   CHILL 4 hours

WHAT YOU NEED

16 Nilla Wafers
1 0.25-ounce envelope unflavored gelatin
2 8-ounce packages cream cheese, softened
⅔ cup sugar
1 teaspoon vanilla extract
2 cups whipped topping
1 cup mini semisweet chocolate chips
1 teaspoon vegetable oil

WHAT YOU DO

1. For crust and cheesecakes, line 16 indents of 2 cupcake pans with foil liners. Coat liners with nonstick spray. Place 1 Nilla Wafer in bottom of each cup.
2. Sprinkle gelatin over ¼ cup water in a glass measuring cup; let soak 1 minute. Microwave 30 seconds to dissolve.
3. Beat cream cheese and sugar in a large bowl until smooth. Beat in vanilla, then fold in whipped topping. While beating on medium speed, add dissolved gelatin in thin stream. Fold in ½ cup of the mini chips. Spoon ¼ cup batter into each cup, smoothing tops.
4. For spiderwebs, combine remaining ½ cup minichips and oil in a microwave-safe bowl. Microwave 1 minute and stir until smooth. Transfer to a resealable plastic bag or piping bag. Snip off a small corner and pipe in a spiral pattern on each cake. Starting at the center, run a thin knife through each spiral to resemble a spiderweb. Refrigerate at least 4 hours. Makes 16 servings.

NO-BAKE SPIDERWEB
CHEESECAKES

BATTY BONBONS

Batty Bonbons

To make these ahead, place finished pops in a single layer in an airtight container. Cover and store in the refrigerator for up to 7 days.

PREP 1 hour FREEZE 30 minutes
CHILL 1 hour

WHAT YOU NEED

18 chocolate sandwich cookies with cream filling
¾ cup pecans, toasted
3 tablespoons flavored liqueur, such as orange or raspberry, or orange juice
2 tablespoons unsweetened cocoa powder
2 tablespoons light-color corn syrup
18 lollipop sticks
12 ounces chocolate-flavor candy coating or semisweet chocolate pieces
    Black sugar pearls or miniature semisweet chocolate pieces

WHAT YOU DO

1. In a large food processor combine cookies and pecans. Cover and process with on-off pulses until cookies are crushed. Add liqueur or orange juice, cocoa powder, and corn syrup. Cover and process until combined.
2. Line a large baking sheet with parchment. Shape cookie mixture into eighteen 1¼-inch balls. Place balls on baking sheet. Insert a lollipop stick into each ball. Freeze for 30 minutes.
3. Melt chocolate-flavor candy coating according to package directions. Working in batches, dip cookie pops into melted candy coating. Allow excess to drip off; place balls on clean trays or baking sheets lined with waxed paper.* Loosely cover and chill 1 hour or until chocolate sets.
4. Draw bat wing outlines on white paper. Line a baking sheet with waxed paper and place the paper wing outlines under the waxed paper to use as templates. Pipe the remaining melted candy coating onto the waxed paper in the shape of 18 pairs of bat wings; chill wings until set.
5. Use melted chocolate-flavor candy coating to attach wings and black sugar pearl eyes to the balls. Allow to set. Makes 18 bonbon pops.

*TIP: If you don't want pops to have a flat side, poke the ends of the lollipop sticks into florist's foam to hold the pops upright until the coating is set.

Grave-Digger Pie

If you're short on time, substitute 3 cups of prepared chocolate pudding for the homemade filling.

PREP 30 minutes COOK 15 minutes
CHILL 4 hours STAND 10 minutes

WHAT YOU NEED

    Nonstick cooking spray
1½ cups finely crushed chocolate wafer cookies (about 25 cookies)
⅓ cup butter, melted
4 egg yolks
1 cup sugar
3 tablespoons cornstarch
2½ cups half-and-half or light cream
3 ounces unsweetened chocolate, chopped
1 tablespoon butter
1½ teaspoons vanilla
1 8-ounce carton frozen extra-creamy whipped dessert topping, thawed
4 ounces semisweet chocolate, chopped
    Chocolate wafer cookies
    Sweetened flaked coconut
    Green food coloring
    Chocolate-filled oblong butter cookies
    White baking chocolate
    Milk chocolate candy bar
    Pumpkin-shape candies

WHAT YOU DO

1. Lightly coat a 9-inch pie plate with nonstick cooking spray; set aside. In a medium bowl stir together 1½ cups crushed chocolate wafer cookies and the ⅓ cup melted butter; press onto the bottom and up the sides of the prepared pie plate. Chill about 1 hour or until firm.
2. Place egg yolks in a small bowl and beat lightly; set aside.
3. In a medium saucepan combine sugar and cornstarch. Gradually stir in half-and-half and unsweetened chocolate. Cook and stir over medium-high heat until thickened and bubbly; reduce heat. Cook and stir for 2 minutes more. Remove saucepan from heat. Gradually stir about 1 cup of the hot filling into the egg yolks in bowl. Add yolk mixture to saucepan. Return to heat and bring to a gentle boil, stirring constantly; reduce heat. Cook and stir for 2 minutes more. Remove from heat. Stir in 1 tablespoon butter and the vanilla. Pour filling into chilled crust and refrigerate for at least 3 hours or until set.
4. Top chilled pie with whipped topping. To decorate, melt semisweet chocolate.* Transfer chocolate into a small resealable plastic freezer bag; snip a small hole in one corner of the bag. On a baking sheet lined with waxed paper, pipe melted chocolate in the shape of a 7- to 8-inch-tall tree. Chill on baking sheet in refrigerator for 1 hour or until chocolate tree is solid.
5. Meanwhile, crush additional wafer cookies; set aside. In a small bowl combine coconut and a drop of green food coloring; mix until color is evenly distributed through coconut. Sprinkle pie with crushed cookie dirt and tinted coconut. With remaining melted semisweet chocolate, pipe epitaphs on oblong cookies. Melt white baking chocolate. Transfer melted white chocolate into a small resealable plastic freezer bag; snip a tiny hole in a corner; pipe epitaphs on pieces of candy bar. Let cookies and candy bar pieces stand at room temperature for 10 to 12 minutes or until set.
6. Decorate top of pie with the chocolate tree, cookie tombstones, milk chocolate tombstones, and pumpkin-shape candies. Refrigerate until serving time. Cut into wedges. Makes 8 servings.

*TIP: To melt chocolate, in a small microwave-safe bowl melt chopped chocolate on high (100% power) for 1 to 1½ minutes, stirring once halfway through melting time. Stir until melted and smooth.

Eerie Outdoor Decor

Decorate your yard with haunting Halloween designs that cast a spooky spell over the whole neighborhood.

For the Birds

One bird: not a big deal. A whole flock of them? That's something a little more scary. Assemble a collection of faux ravens and arrange them in a variety of poses on your fence, porch, banister, deck railing, and even roofline. Secure with cable ties and black duct tape.

Flying Bat Display

Ominously animate your yard with colonies of going-airborne bats. Draw bat shapes onto black foam-core board and cut out; poke two holes into each bat for black cable ties to hold it onto a branch. Stick tall limbs into the ground or into sand-filled buckets. Place the largest bats high on the branches and smaller ones toward the bottom, making sure each cable tie is tight.

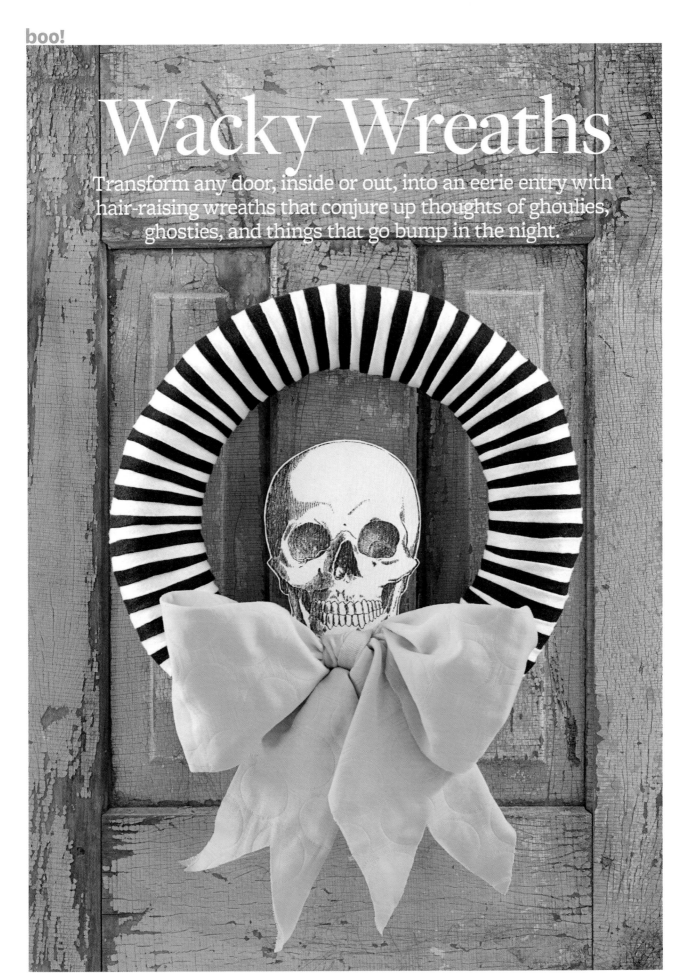

Wacky Wreaths

Transform any door, inside or out, into an eerie entry with hair-raising wreaths that conjure up thoughts of ghoulies, ghosties, and things that go bump in the night.

Skeleton Wreath

Part frightful, part formal, this skull-adorned wreath gets its stripes from overlapping strips of felt. You'll need about 50 each of 10×½-inch pieces of black and white felt. Use straight pins to secure to a 14-inch straw wreath form. Print a free skeleton image from the Internet and coat with decoupage medium; let dry. Use skewers to attach it to the wreath and tie a bow with upholstery fabric for dramatic effect.

Scary Spider Wreath

A bag of inexpensive plastic spiders and a plastic foam wreath are all you need to create a creepy-crawly front door wreath. Simply paint a wreath shape black and hot-glue the spiders to the wreath. And make sure to save space in the center for the mother of all: a big arachnid.

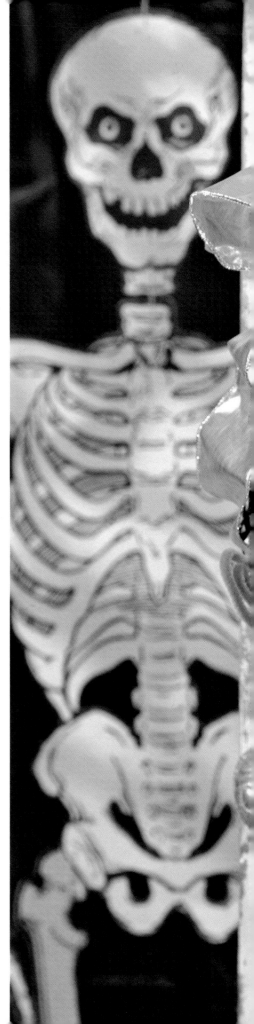

Moss-Filled Halloween Wreath

Make a wreath that looks worn from years of spooky service. Hot-glue faux moss to a foam wreath. Tuck in a few bittersweet branches or seasonal leaves and hot-glue in place. Wire in a raven, mouse, or spider just off center on the wreath; hang using a wide velvet or satin ribbon.

Curl and Swirl

Combine classic Halloween colors—black and orange—with a bit of silver for an easy-to-make a wreath to hang on the front door. For the base, spray-paint a grapevine wreath black and let dry. Shape several orange and silver chenille stems into coils and spirals. Wrap an orange chenille stem around a pencil to make a long spiral. Remove the spiral and tuck it into the wreath, securing under the vines. Make seven spirals and attach them to the wreath. Secure the coils and spirals on the wreath by wrapping the ends around the vines. Cut 2-inch pieces from black chenille stems. Thread a white pony bead on each stem piece; twist to secure and attach to wreath. Continue adding beads between the chenille shapes until the desired look is achieved. Finish with a silver bow.

Feathered Frame

Give your favorite raven a sleek perch. A picture frame wrapped in a feather boa flutters with funereal omens. Display the classic black wreath against a white or gray background.

Spotlight Fright-Night Forms

Suspend ribbon-shrouded wreaths so sun rays and moonbeams showcase their circular silhouettes and satiny sheen. Enhance the otherworldly look by hanging valances cut from newspapers; accent their scallops with "buttons" punched from black paper.

Easy Does It
goodie goodie

Rubber bands in all sizes and colors dress up a plain jar in a hurry. To find wide decorative bands, look in office supply stores. If they are too long for the jar, snip ends, adjust, and hot-glue in place. The fun part is you can change the look of the jar for every season depending on the band colors.

Pail Pal
Check out a scrapbook or crafts store for see-through mini pails. Cut a piece of decorative paper to line the side. Tie on a multiribbon bow with stacked buttons glued to the center for a playful touch.

On a Roll
Crackers get a Halloween makeover with fun papers and ribbons disguising candy-filled paper tubes. To personalize the treat holders, use dimensional alphabet stickers in guests' initials.

Party Bags

Perfect as favors, small bags can hold myriad treats. To make them extra special, fold over the tops after filling. Punch a set of holes through all layers. Use ball chain to hang beads and charms from the flap. Voila! Two gifts in one.

Take-Out Treats

Make a good thing even better. Start with a Halloween-themed take-out box. Once treats are packaged, seal with layered ribbons, taping flat on the bottom. Tie a ribbon bow to the handle and add a large brad accent to the center.

Topped Tin

Tins are a great choice for treats. Hot-glue rickrack around bottom. Cut paper for top; edge it with trim. Glue a button to the center of a ribbon bow and adhere it to the lid with a tag.

Patterns

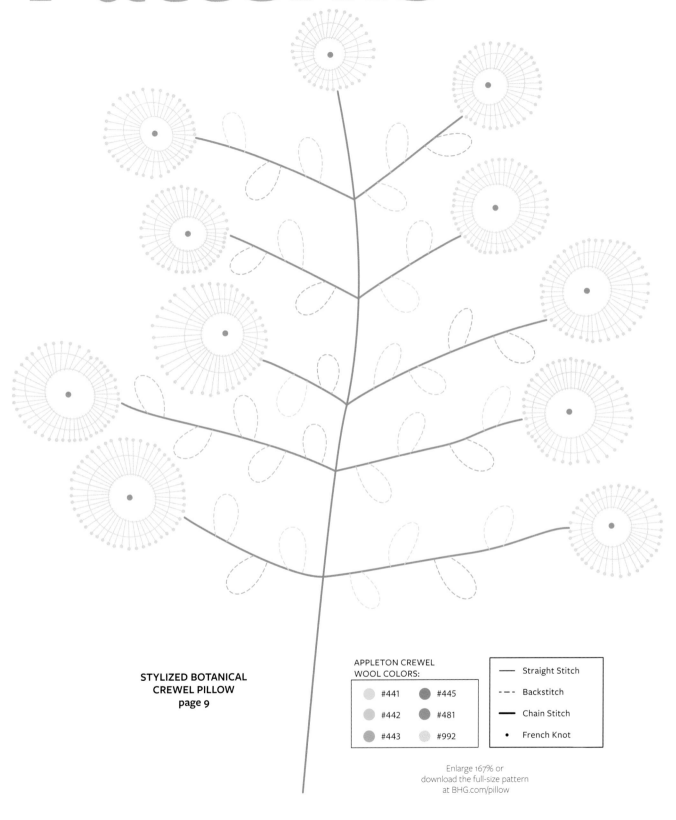

**STYLIZED BOTANICAL
CREWEL PILLOW
page 9**

APPLETON CREWEL
WOOL COLORS:

- #441
- #442
- #443
- #445
- #481
- #992

——	Straight Stitch
- - -	Backstitch
——	Chain Stitch
•	French Knot

Enlarge 167% or
download the full-size pattern
at BHG.com/pillow

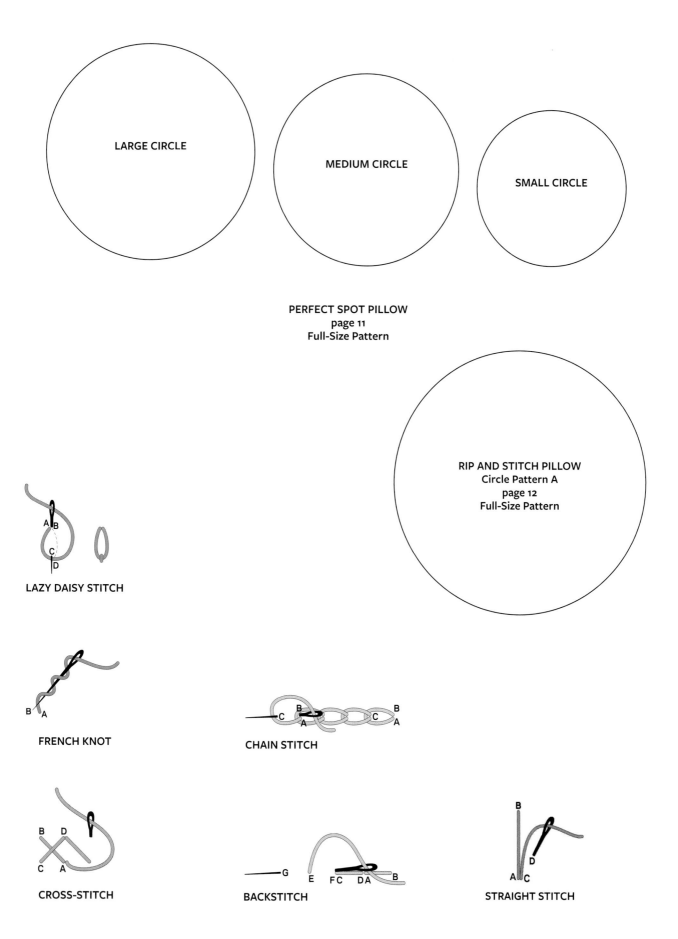

LARGE CIRCLE

MEDIUM CIRCLE

SMALL CIRCLE

PERFECT SPOT PILLOW
page 11
Full-Size Pattern

RIP AND STITCH PILLOW
Circle Pattern A
page 12
Full-Size Pattern

LAZY DAISY STITCH

FRENCH KNOT

CHAIN STITCH

CROSS-STITCH

BACKSTITCH

STRAIGHT STITCH

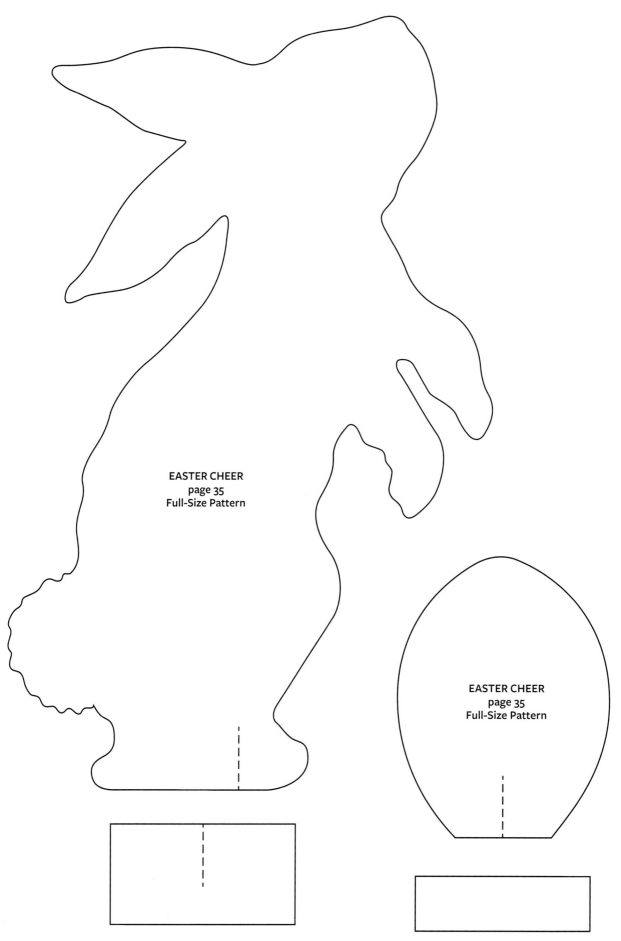

EASTER CHEER
page 35
Full-Size Pattern

EASTER CHEER
page 35
Full-Size Pattern

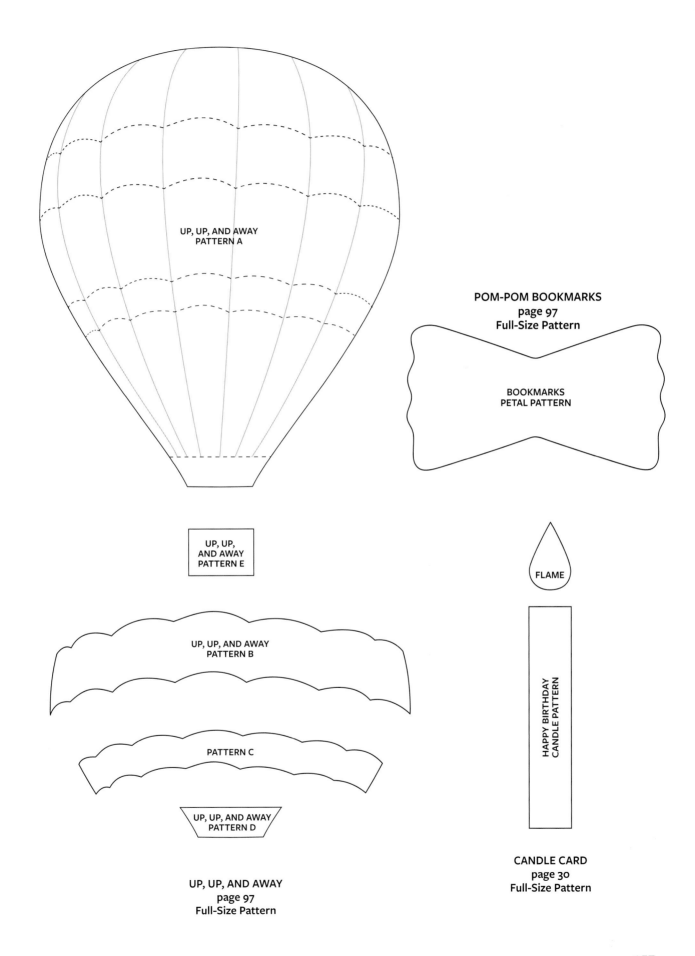

UP, UP, AND AWAY
PATTERN A

POM-POM BOOKMARKS
page 97
Full-Size Pattern

BOOKMARKS
PETAL PATTERN

UP, UP,
AND AWAY
PATTERN E

FLAME

UP, UP, AND AWAY
PATTERN B

PATTERN C

UP, UP, AND AWAY
PATTERN D

HAPPY BIRTHDAY
CANDLE PATTERN

UP, UP, AND AWAY
page 97
Full-Size Pattern

CANDLE CARD
page 30
Full-Size Pattern

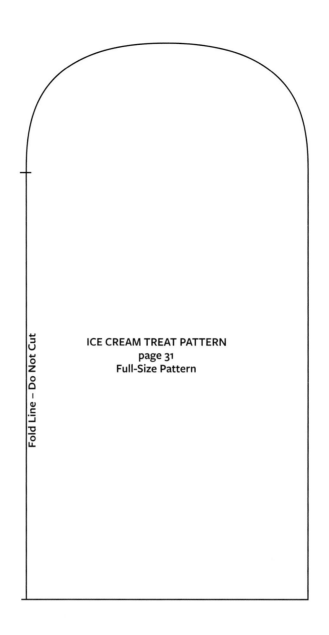

Fold Line – Do Not Cut

ICE CREAM TREAT PATTERN
page 31
Full-Size Pattern

**GET YOUR GHOUL ON
MOUTH AND NOSTRIL PATTERN**
page 123
Full-Size Pattern

Index

index *continued*

CREDITS

Photo Styling
Sue Banker
Cathy Brett

Photography
Jay Wilde
Marty Baldwin